SERIES 63
EXAM STUDY GUIDE 2023 + TEST BANK

SECURITIES INSTITUTE
SECURITIES LICENSING SERIES

The Securities Institute of America proudly publishes world class textbooks, test banks and video training classes for the following Financial Services exams:

    Securities Industry Essentials exam / SIE exam
                Series 3 exam
                Series 4 exam
                Series 6 exam
                Series 7 exam
                Series 9 exam
                Series 10 exam
                Series 22 exam
                Series 24 exam
                Series 26 exam
                Series 39 exam
                Series 57 exam
                Series 63 exam
                Series 65 exam
                Series 66 exam
                Series 79 exam
                Series 99 exam

For more information, visit the website at www.securitiesCE.com.

SERIES 63
EXAM STUDY GUIDE 2023
+ TEST BANK

The Uniform Securities Agent
State Law Examination

The Securities Institute of America, Inc.

Copyright © by The Securities Institute of America, Inc. All rights reserved.

Published by The Securities Institute of America, Inc.

No part of this publication may be reproduced, stored in a retrieval system, or transmitted in any form or by any means, electronic, mechanical, photocopying, recording, scanning, or otherwise, except as permitted under Section 107 or 108 of the 1976 United States Copyright Act, without either the prior written permission of The Securities Institute of America, Inc.

Limit of Liability/Disclaimer of Warranty: While the publisher and author have used their best efforts in preparing this book, they make no representations or warranties with respect to the accuracy or completeness of the contents of this book and specifically disclaim any implied warranties of merchantability or fitness for a particular purpose. No warranty may be created or extended by sales representatives or written sales materials. The advice and strategies contained herein may not be suitable for your situation. You should consult with a professional where appropriate. Neither the publisher nor author shall be liable for any loss of profit or any other commercial damages, including but not limited to special, incidental, consequential, or other damages.

ISBN: 978-1-959462-22-4 (Paperback)

ISBN 978-1-959462-23-1 (ePub)

Printed in the United States of America.
10 9 8 7 6 5 4 3 2 1

Contents

ABOUT THE SERIES 63 EXAM VII

ABOUT THIS BOOK XI

ABOUT THE TEST BANK XIII

ABOUT THE GREENLIGHT GUARANTEE XV

ABOUT THE SECURITIES INSTITUTE OF AMERICA XVII

CHAPTER 1
FEDERAL LAW REVIEW 1

    The Securities Act of 1933 1
    The Prospectus 2
    The Final Prospectus 2
    Misrepresentations 3
    The Securities Exchange Act of 1934 3
    Net Capital Requirement 7
    Customer Coverage 7
    Fidelity Bond 8

The Insider Trading and Securities Fraud Enforcement Act of 1988	8
Firewall	9
The Telephone Consumer Protection Act of 1991	9
National Securities Market Improvement Act of 1996	10
The Uniform Securities Act	11
The Uniform Prudent Investors Act of 1994	12
The Department of Labor Fiduciary Standard	13
The Patriot Act	13
Regulation S-P	14
Identity Theft	15
FINRA Rules on Financial Exploitation of Seniors	16

CHAPTER 2
DEFINITION OF TERMS — 21

Security	21
Person	23
Broker Dealer	24
Pension Consultants	26
Investment Counsel	26
Form ADV	27
Investment Adviser Registration Database (IARD)	28
Investment Adviser Representative	29
Offer/Offer to Sell/Offer to Buy	31
Sale/Sell	32
Guarantee/Guaranteed	32
12B-1 Fees	32
Contumacy	33
Federally Covered Exemption	33
Power of attorney	34
Escheatment	34
Pretest	35

CHAPTER 3
REGISTRATION OF BROKER DEALERS, INVESTMENT ADVISERS, AND AGENTS — 41

Registration of Broker Dealers and Agents	41
Agent Registration	42
Registering Broker Dealers	43
Financial Requirements	44
Broker Dealers on the Premises of Other Financial Institutions	44
Hiring New Employees	45
Resignation of a Registered Representative	46
Maintaining Qualifications Program	47
Registering Agents	48
Canadian Firms and Agents	50
Investment Adviser Registration	50
The National Securities Market Improvement Act of 1996/The Coordination Act	51
Investment Adviser Representative	52
Investment Adviser Registration	52
Capital Requirements	53
Exams	54
Advertising and Sales Literature	54
Brochure Delivery	55
Wrap Accounts	56
Pretest	57

CHAPTER 4
SECURITIES REGISTRATION, EXEMPT SECURITIES, AND EXEMPT TRANSACTIONS — 63

Exempt Securities	63
Securities Registration	64
Registration of IPOs Through Coordination	64
Registration Through Notice Filing	65
Registration of Non-Established Issuers/Registration Through Qualification	65
Exempt Securities/Federally Covered Exemption	67
Exempt Transactions	68
Rule 147 Intrastate Offering	71
Pretest	73

CHAPTER 5
PROFESSIONAL CONDUCT AND PROHIBITED AND FRAUDULENT ACTIONS 79

- Fraud — 79
- Professional Conduct — 80
- Suitability — 80
- Market Manipulation — 82
- Customer Complaints — 83
- The Role of the Investment Adviser — 83
- Additional Compensation for an Investment Adviser — 84
- Agency Cross Transactions — 84
- Disclosures by an Investment Adviser — 84
- Investment Adviser Contracts — 86
- SEC Marketing Rules for Investment Advisers — 86
- Private Investment Companies/Hedge Funds — 88
- Fulcrum Fees — 89
- Soft Dollars — 89
- Borrowing and Lending Money — 91
- Free Services — 91
- Pretest — 93

CHAPTER 6
THE STATE SECURITIES ADMINISTRATOR AND THE UNIFORM SECURITIES ACT 101

- Actions by the State Securities Administrator — 101
- Cancellation of a Registration — 102
- Withdrawal of a Registration — 103
- Actions Against an Issuer of Securities — 103
- Rule Changes — 103
- Administrative Orders — 103
- Interpretive Opinions — 105
- Administrative Records — 105
- Investigations — 106
- Civil and Criminal Penalties — 106

Contents

Jurisdiction of the State Securities Administrator	107
Administrator's Jurisdiction over Securities Transactions	108
Radio, Television, and Newspaper Distribution	110
Right of Rescission	111
Statute of Limitations	111
Pretest	113

ANSWER KEYS   119

GLOSSARY OF EXAM TERMS   127

About the Series 63 Exam

Congratulations! You are on your way to becoming a registered representative licensed to conduct securities business in all states that require the Series 63. The Series 63 exam will be presented in a 60-question multiple-choice format. Each candidate will have one hour and 15 minutes to complete the exam. A score of 72% or higher is required to pass.

The Series 63 is as much a knowledge test as it is a reading test. The writers and instructors at The Securities Institute have developed the Series 63 textbook, exam prep software, and videos to ensure that you have the knowledge required to pass the test and to make sure that you are confident in the application of the knowledge during the exam.

> IMPORTANT **EXAM NOTE**
>
> The Series 63 exam is based on the provisions of the Uniform Securities Act not on any of the amendments enacted by any particular state or state securities administrator. The Uniform Securities Act may be referred to as the USA or as the Act. Test takers should treat these terms as interchangeable.

TAKING THE SERIES 63 EXAM

The Series 63 exam is presented in multiple-choice format on a touch-screen computer known as the PROCTOR system. No computer skills are required, and candidates will find that the test screen works in the same way as an ordinary ATM. Each test is made up of 60 questions that are randomly chosen from a test bank containing several thousand questions. The test has a time limit of one hour and 15 minutes and is designed to provide enough time for all candidates to complete the exam. Each Series 63 exam will have five additional questions that do not count towards the final score. The Series 63 comprises questions that focus on the following areas:

State-Registered and Federal Covered Advisers	3 questions	5%
Regulation of Investment Adviser Representatives	3 questions	5%
Regulations of Broker Dealers	9 questions	15%
Regulations of Agents of Broker Dealers	9 questions	15%
Regulation of Securities and Issuers	3 questions	5%
Remedies and Administrative Provisions	6 questions	10%
Communications with Customers and Prospects	12 questions	20%
Ethical Practices and Obligations	15 questions	25%

HOW TO PREPARE FOR THE SERIES 63 EXAM

For most candidates, the combination of reading the textbook, watching the videos, and using the exam prep software is enough to successfully complete the exam. It is recommended that the candidate spend at least 30 hours preparing for the exam by reading the textbook, underlining key points, watching the video class, and completing as many practice questions as possible. We recommend that candidates schedule their exam no more than one week after completing their Series 63 exam prep.

Test-Taking Tips

- ☐ Read the full question before answering.
- ☐ Identify what the question is asking.
- ☐ Identify key words and phrases.
- ☐ Watch out for hedge clauses, for example, *except* and *not*.
- ☐ Eliminate wrong answers.
- ☐ Identify synonymous terms.
- ☐ Be wary of changing answers.

WHY DO I NEED TO TAKE THE SERIES 63 EXAM?

In order to conduct securities business, most states require that an agent successfully complete the Series 63, in addition to obtaining a Series 6, 7, or 79 registration.

WHAT SCORE IS NEEDED TO PASS THE EXAM?

A score of 72% or higher is needed to pass the Series 63 exam.

ARE THERE ANY PREREQUISITES FOR THE SERIES 63?

A candidate is not required to have any other professional qualifications prior to taking the Series 63 exam.

HOW DO I SCHEDULE AN EXAM?

Ask your firm's principal to schedule the exam for you or to supply you with a list of test centers in your area. If you are not with a member firm, you may obtain a Form U10 from the North American Securities Administrators Association (NASAA) to make an appointment. The Series 63 exam may be taken any day that the exam center is open.

WHAT MUST I TAKE TO THE EXAM CENTER?

A picture ID is required. All other materials will be provided, including a calculator and scratch paper.

HOW SOON WILL I RECEIVE THE RESULTS OF THE EXAM?

The exam will be graded as soon as you answer your final question and hit the Submit for Grading button. It will take only a few minutes to get your results. Your grade will appear on the computer screen, and you will be given a paper copy from the exam center.

If you do not pass the test, you will need to wait 30 days before taking it again. If you do not pass on the second try, you will need to wait another 30 days. If you fail a third time, you are required to wait six months to take the test again.

x

About This Book

The writers and instructors at The Securities Institute have developed the Series 63 textbook, exam prep software, and videos to ensure that you have the knowledge required to pass the test, and to make sure that you are confident in the application of the knowledge during the exam. The writers and instructors at The Securities Institute are subject-matter experts as well as Series 63 test experts. We understand how the test is written, and our proven test-taking techniques can dramatically improve your results.

Each chapter includes notes, tips, examples, and case studies with key information, hints for taking the exam, and additional insight into the topics. Each chapter ends with a practice test, to ensure that you have mastered the concepts before moving on to the next topic.

About the Test Bank

This book is accompanied by a test bank of hundreds of questions to further reinforce the concepts and information presented here. The test bank is provided to help students who have purchased our book from a traditional bookstore or from an online retailer such as Amazon. If you have purchased this textbook as part of a package from our website containing the full version of the software, you are all set and simply need to use the login instructions that were emailed to you at the time of purchase. Otherwise to access the test bank please email your purchase receipt to sales@securitiesce.com and we will activate your account. This test bank provides a small sample of the questions and features that are contained in the full version of the exam prep software.

If you have not purchased the full version of the exam prep software with this book, we highly recommend it to ensure that you have mastered the knowledge required for your exam. To purchase the exam prep software for this exam, visit The Securities Institute of America online at: www.securitiesce.com or call 877-218-1776.

About The Greenlight Guarantee

Quite simply the Greenlight guarantee is as follows:
Pass our Greenlight exam within 5 days of your actual exam, and if you do not pass we will refund the money you paid to The Securities Institute. If you only have access to the Limited Test Bank through the purchase of this textbook, you may upgrade your online account for a small fee to include the Greenlight exam and receive the full benefits of our greenlight money back pass guarantee.

About The Securities Institute of America

The Securities Institute of America, Inc. Helps thousands of securities and insurance professionals build successful careers in the financial services industry every year. In more than 25 years we have helped students pass more than 400,000 exams. Our securities training options include:

- Classroom training

- Private tutoring

- Interactive online video training classes

- State-of-the-art exam prep test banks

- Printed textbooks

- ebooks

- Real-time tracking and reporting for managers and training directors

As a result, you can choose a securities training solution that matches your skill level, learning style, and schedule. Regardless of the format you choose, you can be sure that our securities training courses are relevant, tested, and designed to help you succeed. It is the experience of our instructors and the quality of our materials that make our courses requested by name at some of the largest financial services firms in the world.

To contact The Securities Institute of America, visit us on the Web at: www.securitiesce.com or call 877-218-1776.

CHAPTER 1

Federal Law Review

> **INTRODUCTION**
>
> Although the Series 63 exam is a state-based exam, a full understanding of federal securities laws is required. All federal securities laws have a year attached to them that corresponds with the year the law was enacted.

THE SECURITIES ACT OF 1933

The Securities Act of 1933 was the first major piece of securities industry regulation, which was brought about largely as a result of the stock market crash of 1929. Other laws were also enacted to help prevent another meltdown of the nation's financial system, such as the Securities Exchange Act of 1934, which will be discussed later.

The Securities Act of 1933 regulates the primary market. The primary market consists exclusively of transactions between issuers of securities and investors. In a primary market transaction, the issuer of the securities receives the proceeds from the sale of the securities. The Securities Act of 1933 requires nonexempt issuers, typically corporate issuers, to file a registration statement with the Securities and Exchange Commission (SEC). The SEC will review the registration statement for a minimum of 20 days. During this time, known as the cooling-off period, no sales of securities may take place. If the SEC requires additional information regarding the offering, the SEC may issue a deficiency letter or a stop order that will extend the cooling-off period beyond the original 20 days. The cooling-off period will continue until the SEC has received all of the information it has requested. The registration statement, formally known as an S1, is the issuer's full disclosure document for the registration of the securities with the SEC.

THE PROSPECTUS

While the SEC is reviewing the securities' registration statement, registered representatives are very limited as to what they may do with regard to the new issue. During the cooling-off period, the only thing a registered representative may do is obtain indications on interest from clients by providing them with a preliminary prospectus, also known as a red herring. The term "red herring" originated from the fact that all preliminary prospectuses must have a statement printed in red ink on the front cover stating, "These securities have not yet become registered with the SEC and therefore may not be sold." An indication of interest is an investor's or broker dealer's statement that it may be interested in purchasing the securities being offered. The preliminary prospectus contains most of the same information that will be contained in the final prospectus except for the offering price and the proceeds to the issuer. All information contained in a preliminary prospectus is subject to change or revision. The preliminary prospectus must be delivered to investors in hard copy.

THE FINAL PROSPECTUS

All purchasers of new issues must be given a final prospectus before any sales may be allowed. The final prospectus serves as the issuer's full-disclosure document for the purchaser of the securities. If the issuer has filed a prospectus with the SEC and the prospectus can be viewed on the SEC's website, a prospectus will be deemed to have been provided to the investor through the "access equals delivery" rule. Once the issuer's registration statement becomes effective, the final prospectus must include the following:

- Type and description of the securities
- Price of the securities
- Use of the proceeds
- Underwriter's discount
- Date of offering
- Type and description of underwriting
- Business history of issuer

- Biographical data for company officers and directors
- Information regarding large stockholders
- Company financial data
- Risks to purchaser
- Legal matters concerning the company
- SEC disclaimer

SEC DISCLAIMER

The SEC reviews the issuer's registration statement and the prospectus but does not guarantee the accuracy or adequacy of the information. The following SEC disclaimer must appear on the cover of all prospectuses: "These securities have not been approved or disapproved by the SEC nor have any representations been made about the accuracy or the adequacy of the information."

MISREPRESENTATIONS

Financial relief for misrepresentations made under the Securities Act of 1933 is available for purchasers of any security that is sold under a prospectus that is found to contain false or misleading statements. Purchasers of the security may be entitled to seek financial relief from any or all of the following:

1. The issuer.
2. The underwriters.
3. Officers and directors.
4. All parties who signed the registration statement.
5. Accountants and attorneys who helped prepare the registration statement.

THE SECURITIES EXCHANGE ACT OF 1934

The Securities Exchange Act of 1934 was the second major piece of legislation that resulted from the market crash of 1929. The Securities Exchange Act of 1934 regulates the secondary market, which consists of investor-to-investor transactions. All transactions between two investors that are executed on any of the exchanges or in the over-the-counter (OTC) market are secondary market transactions. In a secondary market transaction, the selling security holder receives the money, not the issuing corporation. The Securities Exchange Act of 1934 also regulates all individuals and firms that conduct business in the securities industry. The Securities Exchange Act of 1934:

- Created the SEC.
- Requires registration of broker dealers and agents.
- Regulates the exchanges and FINRA.
- Requires net capital for broker dealers.
- Regulates short sales.
- Regulates insider transactions.
- Requires public companies to solicit proxies.
- Requires segregation of customer and firm assets.
- Authorizes the Federal Reserve Board to regulate the extension of credit for securities purchases under Regulation T.
- Regulates the handling of client accounts.

THE SECURITIES AND EXCHANGE COMMISSION (SEC)

One of the biggest components of the Securities Exchange Act of 1934 was the creation of the SEC. The SEC is the ultimate securities industry authority, and it is a government body. Five commissioners are appointed to five-year terms by the president, and each must be approved by the Senate. The SEC is neither a self-regulatory organization (SRO) nor a designated examining authority (DEA). A self-regulatory organization regulates its own members, such as the New York Stock Exchange (NYSE) or FINRA. A DEA inspects a broker dealer's books and records; it can also be the NYSE or FINRA. All broker dealers, exchanges, agents, and securities must register with the SEC. All exchanges are required to file a registration statement with the SEC that includes the articles of incorporation, bylaws, and constitution. All new rules and regulations adopted by the exchanges must be disclosed to the SEC as soon as they are enacted. Issuers of securities with more than 500 shareholders and with assets exceeding $5,000,000 must register with the SEC, file quarterly and annual reports, and solicit proxies from stockholders. A broker dealer that conducts business with the public must register with the SEC and maintain a certain level of financial solvency, known as net capital. All broker dealers are required to forward a financial statement to all customers of the firm. Additionally, all employees of the broker dealer involved in securities sales who have access to cash and securities or who supervise employees must be fingerprinted.

EXTENSION OF CREDIT

The Securities Act of 1934 gave the authority to the Federal Reserve Board to regulate the extension of credit by broker dealers for the purchase of securities by their customers. The following is a list of the regulations of the different lenders and the regulation that gave the Federal Reserve Board the authority to govern their activities:

- Regulation T: Broker dealers
- Regulation U: Banks
- Regulation G: All other financial institutions

PUBLIC UTILITIES HOLDING COMPANY ACT OF 1935

The Public Utilities Holding Company Act of 1935 regulates all companies that are in business to provide retail distribution of gas and electric power. Because the companies are regulated by this act, their securities are exempt from state registration requirements.

THE MALONEY ACT OF 1938

The Maloney Act of 1938 was an amendment to the Securities Exchange Act of 1934 that allowed the creation of the NASD. The NASD (now FINRA) is the SRO for the OTC market. Its purpose is to regulate the broker dealers that conduct business in the OTC market. FINRA is organized into four major bylaws. They are:

1. The Rules of Fair Practice.
2. The Uniform Practice Code.
3. The Code of Procedure.
4. The Code of Arbitration.

THE TRUST INDENTURE ACT OF 1939

The Trust Indenture Act of 1939 requires that corporate bond issues in excess of $10,000,000 that are to be repaid during a term in excess of one year issue a trust indenture for the issue. The trust indenture is a contract between the issuer and the trustee. The trustee acts on behalf of all of the bondholders and ensures that the issuer is in compliance with all of the promises and covenants made to the bondholders. The trustee is appointed by the corporation and is usually a bank or a trust company. The Trust Indenture Act of 1939 only applies to corporate issuers. Both federal and municipal issuers are exempt.

INVESTMENT ADVISERS ACT OF 1940

The Investment Advisers Act of 1940 regulates industry professionals who charge a fee for the advice they offer to clients. The Investment Advisers Act sets forth registration requirements for advisers as well as disclosure requirements relating to the adviser's:

- Methods of recommendations
- Types of securities recommended
- Professional background and qualifications
- Fees to be charged
- Method for computing and charging fees
- Types of clients

INVESTMENT COMPANY ACT OF 1940

The Investment Company Act of 1940 regulates companies that are in business to invest or reinvest money for the benefit of its investors. The Investment Company Act sets forth registration requirements for the three types of investment companies. They are:

1. Management investment companies.
2. Unit investment trusts (UITs).
3. Face-amount companies (FACs).

SECURITIES INVESTOR PROTECTION CORPORATION ACT OF 1970 (SIPC)

The Securities Investor Protection Corporation (SIPC) is a government-sponsored corporation that provides protection to customers in the event of a broker dealer's failure. All broker dealers that are registered with the SEC are required to be SIPC members. All broker dealers are required to pay annual dues to SIPC's insurance fund to cover losses due to broker dealer failure. If a broker dealer fails to pay its SIPC assessment, it may not transact business until it is paid.

NET CAPITAL REQUIREMENT

All broker dealers are required to maintain a certain level of net capital in order to ensure that they are financially solvent. A broker dealer's capital requirement is contingent on the type of business that it conducts. The larger and more complex the firm's business, the greater the net capital requirement. Should a firm fall below its net capital requirement, it is deemed to be insolvent, and SIPC will petition in court to have a trustee appointed to liquidate the firm and protect the customers. The trustee must be a disinterested party; once the trustee is appointed, the firm may not conduct business or try to conceal any assets.

CUSTOMER COVERAGE

SIPC protects customers of a brokerage firm in much the same way that the Federal Deposit Insurance Corporation (FDIC) protects customers of banks. SIPC covers customer losses that result from broker dealer failure, not market losses. SIPC covers customers for up to $500,000 per separate customer. Of the $500,000, up to $250,000 may be in cash. Most broker dealers carry additional private insurance to cover larger accounts, but SIPC is the industry-funded insurance and is required by all broker dealers. The following are examples of separate customers:

Customer	Securities Market Value	Cash	SIPC Coverage
Mr. Jones	$320,000	$75,000	All
Mr. & Mrs. Jones	$290,000	$90,000	All
Mrs. Jones	$397,000	$82,000	All

All of the accounts shown would be considered separate customers, and SIPC would cover the entire value of the accounts. If an account has in excess of $250,000 in cash, the individual would not be covered for any amount exceeding $250,000 in cash and would become a general creditor for the rest. SIPC does not consider a margin account and a cash account as separate customers, and the customer would be covered for the maximum of $500,000. SIPC does not offer coverage for commodities contracts, and all member firms must display the SIPC sign in the lobby of the firm.

FIDELITY BOND

All SIPC members are required to obtain a fidelity bond to protect customers in the event of employee dishonesty. Some things that a fidelity bond will insure against are check forgery and fraudulent trading. The minimum amount of the fidelity bond is $25,000; however, large firms are often required to carry a higher amount.

THE INSIDER TRADING AND SECURITIES FRAUD ENFORCEMENT ACT OF 1988

The Insider Trading and Securities Fraud Enforcement Act of 1988 set forth guidelines and controls for the use and dissemination of nonpublic material information. Nonpublic information is information that is not known by people outside of the company. Material information is information regarding a situation or development that will materially affect the company in the present or future. It is not only just for insiders to have this type of information, but it is required for them to do their jobs effectively. It is, however, unlawful for an insider to use this information to profit from a forthcoming move in the stock price. An insider is defined as any officer, director, 10% stockholder, or anyone who is in possession of nonpublic material information, as well as the spouse of any such person. Additionally, it is unlawful for the insider to divulge any of this information to any outside party.

Trading on inside information has always been a violation of the Securities Exchange Act of 1934, but the Insider Trading Act prescribed penalties for violators, which include:

- A fine of the greater of 300% of the amount of the gain or 300% of the amount of the loss avoided, or $1,000,000 for the person who acts on the information
- A fine of up to $1,000,000 for the person who divulges the information
- Insider traders may be sued by the affected parties
- Criminal prosecutions

Information becomes public information once it has been disseminated over public media. The SEC will pay a reward of up to 10% to informants who turn in individuals who trade on inside information. In addition to the insiders already listed, the following are also considered insiders:

- Accountants
- Attorneys
- Investment bankers

FIREWALL

Broker dealers who act as underwriters and investment bankers for corporate clients must have access to information regarding the company in order to advise the company properly. The broker dealer must ensure that no inside information is passed between its investment banking department and its retail trading department. The broker dealer is required to physically separate these divisions by a firewall. The broker dealer must maintain written supervisory procedures to adequately guard against the wrongful use or dissemination of inside information.

THE TELEPHONE CONSUMER PROTECTION ACT OF 1991

The Telephone Consumer Protection Act of 1991 regulates how telemarketing calls are made by businesses. Telemarketing calls that are designed to have consumers invest in or purchase goods, services, or property must adhere to the strict guidelines of the act. All firms must:

- Call only between the hours of 8 a.m. and 9 p.m. in the customer's time zone.
- Maintain a Do-Not-Call list. Individuals placed on the Do-Not-Call list may not be contacted by anyone at the firm for five years.
- Give the prospect the firm's name, address, and phone number when soliciting.
- Follow adequate policies and procedures to maintain a Do-Not-Call list.
- Train representatives on calling policies and use of the Do-Not-Call list.
- Ensure that any fax solicitations have the firm's name, address, and phone number.
- Ensure that the name of the firm and phone number are displayed on caller ID.

EXEMPTION FROM THE TELEPHONE CONSUMER PROTECTION ACT OF 1991

The following are exempt from the Telephone Consumer Protection Act of 1991:

- Calls to existing customers
- Calls to a delinquent debtor
- Calls from a religious or nonprofit organization

Calls may be made prior to 8 a.m. or after 9 p.m. to places of business. The time regulation only relates to contacting noncustomers at home.

NATIONAL SECURITIES MARKET IMPROVEMENT ACT OF 1996

The National Securities Market Improvement Act of 1996, also known as the Coordination Act, eliminated the duplication of effort among state and federal regulators. Some of the key points of the act include:

- Federal law supersedes state law.
- Registration of investment advisers.
- Capital requirements.
- Industry competition.

The National Securities Market Improvement Act of 1996 ensured that no action by any state or political subdivision could impose laws or requirements upon any broker dealer that differed from or are in addition to those of the Securities Exchange Act of 1934 relating to:

- Capital requirements.
- Recordkeeping.
- Financial reporting.
- Margin.
- Custody.

The National Securities Market Improvement Act of 1996 also set forth that the states did not have any authority to regulate investment advisory firms that are federally registered. However, the states may require an investment advisory representative of a federally registered investment adviser to register with the state.

THE UNIFORM SECURITIES ACT

In the early half of the twentieth century, state securities regulators developed rules and regulations for transacting securities business within their states. The result was regulations that varied widely from state to state. The Uniform Securities Act (USA) laid out model legislation for all states in an effort to make each state's rules and regulations more uniform and easier to address. The USA, or the Act, sets minimum qualifications and standards for each state securities administrator. The state securities administrator is the top securities regulator within the state. The state securities administrator may be the attorney general or it may be an individual appointed specifically to that post. The USA also:

- Prohibits the state securities administrator from using the post for personal benefit or from disclosing information.
- Gives the state securities administrator authority to enforce the rules of the USA within that state.
- Gives the administrator the ability to set certain registration requirements for broker dealers, agents, and investment advisers.
- Allows administrators to set fee and testing requirements.
- Permits administrators to suspend or revoke the state registration of a broker dealer, agent, investment adviser, a security, or a security's exemption from registration.
- Sets civil and criminal penalties for violators.

The state-based laws set forth by the USA are also known as blue sky laws. Collectively the State Securities Administrators from each state make up the North American Securities Administrators Association or NASAA. The North America Securities Administrators' Association is a body of state regulators each of whom is responsible for administering the provisions of the Uniform Securities Act within their state. Together they make up an advisory committee that refines and amends the Uniform Securities Act through the adoption of module rules and policy statements. NASAA is also responsible for creating the content tested on the Series 63, 65, and 66 exams. Some of the more testable concepts relating to NASAA's model rules and policy statements include the following:

- Policy statement detailing dishonest and unethical business practices of broker dealers and agents
- Policy statement relating to dishonest sales practices relating to the sale of investment company products by broker dealers and agents
- Policy statement detailing requirements for broker dealers conducting business on the premises of other financial (banking) institutions
- Model Rule covering unethical business practices of investment advisers
- Model Rule detailing requirements for investment advisers who maintain custody of client funds

THE UNIFORM PRUDENT INVESTORS ACT OF 1994

The Uniform Prudent Investors Act of 1994, or UPIA, sets the basic standards by which all investment professionals acting in a fiduciary capacity must abide. The UPIA updates the requirements and definitions of prudent standards in light of the application of modern portfolio theory and the advancement in the understanding of the behavior of capital markets. The UPIA laid out five fundamental changes in the approach to prudent investing for investment professionals acting in a fiduciary capacity. Those changes are:

1. The main consideration of a fiduciary is the management and trade off between risk and reward.
2. The standard of prudence for each investment will be viewed in relationship to the overall portfolio rather than as a standalone investment.
3. The rules regarding diversification have become part of the definition of prudent investing.
4. The restrictions from investing in various types of investments have been removed, and the trustee may invest in anything that is appropriate in light of the objectives of the trust and that is in line with other requirements of prudent investing.
5. The rules against delegating the duties of the trustee have been removed, and the trustee may now delegate investment functions subject to safeguards.

THE DEPARTMENT OF LABOR FIDUCIARY STANDARD

The Department of Labor has enacted significant new legislation for financial professionals who service and maintain retirement accounts for clients. These new rules subject financial professionals to higher fiduciary standards. These standards require financial professionals to place the interest of the client ahead of the interest of the broker dealer or investment advisory firm. Professionals who service retirement accounts are still permitted to earn commissions and/or a fee based on the assets in the account and may still offer proprietary products to investors. However the rule requires that the client receive significant disclosures relating to the fees and costs associated with the servicing of the account. Simply charging the lowest fee will not ensure compliance with the fiduciary standard. Both the firm and the individual servicing the account must put the interests of the client ahead of their own. Broker dealers and advisory firms must establish written supervisory procedures and training programs designed to supervise and educate their personnel on the new requirements for retirement accounts. Many representatives will now be required to obtain the Series 65 or Series 66 license to comply with the new Department of Labor rules. These rules are hotly debated and subject to change.

THE PATRIOT ACT

The Patriot Act, as incorporated in the Bank Secrecy Act, requires broker dealers to have written policies and procedures designed to detect suspicious activity. The firm must designate a principal to ensure compliance with the firm's policies and to train firm personnel. The firm is required to file a Suspicious Activity Report for any transaction of more than $5,000 that appears questionable. The firm must file the report within 30 days of identifying any suspicious activity. Anti-money-laundering rules require that all firms implement a customer identification program to ensure that the firm knows the true identity of their customers. All customers who open an account with the firm, as well as individuals with trading authority, are subject to this rule. The firm must ensure that its customers do not appear on any list of known or suspected terrorists. A firm's anti-money-laundering program must be approved by senior management. All records relating to the SAR filing including a copy of the SAR report must be maintained by the firm for 5 years.

The money laundering process begins with the placement of the funds. This is when the money is deposited in an account with the broker dealer.

The second step of the laundering process is known as layering. The layering process will consist of multiple deposits in amounts less than $10,000. The funds will often be drawn from different financial institutions; this is also known as structuring. The launderers will then purchase and sell securities in the account. The integration of the proceeds back into the banking system completes the process. At this point, the launderers may use the money to purchase goods and services and they appear to have come from legitimate sources. Firms must also identify the customers who open the account and must make sure that they are not conducting business with anyone on the OFAC list. This list is maintained by the Treasury Department Office of Foreign Assets Control. It consists of known and suspected terrorists, criminals, and members of pariah nations. Individuals and entities who appear on this list are known as Specially Designated Nationals and Blocked Persons. Conducting business with anyone on this list is strictly prohibited. Registered representatives who aid in the laundering of money are subject to prosecution and face up to 20 years in prison and a $500,000 fine per transaction. The representative does not even have to be involved in the scheme or even know about it to be prosecuted.

FinCEN is a bureau of the U.S. Department of the Treasury. FinCEN's Imission is to safeguard the financial system and guard against money laundering and promote national security. FinCEN collects, receives, and maintains financial transactions data; analyzes and disseminates that data for law enforcement purposes; and builds global cooperation with counterpart organizations in other countries and with international bodies. FinCEN will email a list of individuals and entities to a designated principal every few weeks. The principal is required to check the list against the firm's customer list. If a match is found the firm must notify FinCEN within 14 calendar days.

REGULATION S-P

Regulation S-P requires that the firm maintain adequate procedures to protect the financial information of its customers. Firms must guard against unauthorized access to customer financial information and must employ policies to ensure its safety. Special concerns arise over the ability of a person to "hack" into a firm's customer database by gaining unauthorized access. Firms must develop and maintain specific safeguards for their computer systems and Wi-Fi access.

Regulation S-P was derived from the privacy rules of the Gramm-Leach-Bliley Act. A firm must deliver:

- An initial privacy notice to customers when the account is opened.
- An annual privacy notice to all customers.

The annual privacy notice may be delivered electronically via the firm's website, as long as the customer has agreed to receive it electronically in writing and it is clearly displayed. The privacy notice must describe the type of information that is collected and the type of nonaffiliated parties with whom it may be shared. Regulation S-P also states that a firm may not disclose nonpublic personal information to nonaffiliated companies for clients who have opted out of the list. The method by which a client may opt out may not be unreasonable. It is considered unreasonable to require a customer to write a letter to opt out. Reasonable methods are emails or a toll-free number. The rule also differentiates between who is a customer and who is a consumer. A customer is anyone who has an ongoing relationship with the firm (i.e., has an account). A consumer is someone who is providing information to the firm and is considering becoming a customer or who has purchased a product from the firms and has no other contact with the firm. The firm must give the privacy notice to consumers prior to sharing any nonpublic information with a nonaffiliated company.

> **TAKENOTE!**
>
> A client of a brokerage firm may not opt out of the sharing of information with an affiliated company.

Regulation S-AM prohibits broker dealers from soliciting business based upon information received from affiliated third parties unless the potential marketing had been clearly disclosed to the potential customer, and the potential customer was provided an opportunity to opt out and did not opt out.

IDENTITY THEFT

The fraudulent practice of identity theft may be used by criminals in an attempt to obtain access to the assets or credit of another person. The Federal

Trade Commission (FTC) requires banks and broker dealers to establish and maintain written identity theft prevention programs. A broker dealer's written supervisory procedures manual must reference its identity theft program. The program must be designed to detect red flags relating to the known suspicious activity employed during an attempt at identity theft. The identity theft prevention program should be designed to allow the firm to respond quickly to any attempted identity theft to mitigate any potential damage.

FINRA RULES ON FINANCIAL EXPLOITATION OF SENIORS

While many people are living active and productive lives well into their eighties and beyond, FINRA has enacted rules designed to protect the financial interests of seniors who are 65 or older. FINRA is particularly concerned about clients being taken advantage of by unscrupulous or otherwise self-serving people. Registered representatives should have a clear understanding of the financial needs, resources, and behavior of their clients. This is specifically important when dealing with older clients who may require the assets to meet their current financial needs, and who can fall victim to bad actors. Registered representatives should be particularly concerned with any requests to withdraw money from an account that is outside the normal actions of the client.

EXAMPLE

Sally is a retired school administrator who is 83 years old and is living on her assets. Sally and her late husband had planned well for their retirement. She has the proceeds from her husband's life insurance policy and a significant savings and retirement account, as well as her social security. Sally has been a client of your firm for 10 years and generally moves $1,800 to $2,000 per month from her brokerage account to her checking account. Twice per year she travels and moves $5,000 to her checking account to pay her travel expenses. One day Sally calls up and says she needs $35,000 wired to an out-of-state bank account. When the agent inquires what this is for, Sally says her friend has told her of an investment opportunity in real estate that she would like to take advantage of. When the agent inquiries about the opportunity, the details Sally provides do not sound right to the agent.

ANALYSIS
This is a serious red flag, and in this situation the agent has a significant conflict. On the one hand, the agent is required to do as the client requests.

On the other, the agent feels a duty to protect the client and senses that their client may be the victim of senior exploitation. Even discussing the matter with a principal of the firm is not enough to determine if the client is being taken advantage of.

FINRA's rules allow broker dealers to withhold distributions to senior clients for 15 business days in cases of suspected financial exploitation. Disbursements to pay bills and other payments made in the normal course of business will be permitted while the hold is in place, so long as they are not deemed suspicious. During this time, the broker dealer should investigate the client's request and obtain as much information regarding the receiving party as they can. To further protect seniors, broker dealers should obtain the name and contact information of a "trusted contact" for senior clients. The firm in very limited circumstances may contact the trusted contact to inquire about requests to withdraw money when financial exploitation is suspected. If the trusted contact or any party with authority over the account is potentially involved in the exploitation of the account holder, the suspected party will not be notified of the hold. The firm may also contact the person to inquire as to the welfare of the client and to inquire as to the identity of any individual who may hold power of attorney or who may be named as executor of the client's will. If the firm at the end of 15 business days has gathered information relating to the request that indicates that this is a case of financial exploitation, the firm may withhold the funds for another 10 business days. The firm should share their findings with the National Center for Elder Abuse as well as with law enforcement. At the conclusion of the 25 day hold, if the firm still has reasonable grounds to suspect that the client is the subject of elder abuse, the firm may continue the hold for an additional 30 business days. As a result, the total number of days a member is allowed to place a hold on a request to distribute funds in a single payment or in a series of payments is 55 business days.

REGULATION BEST INTEREST

Regulation Best Interest (Reg BI) was adopted by the SEC in June of 2019 as an amendment to the Securities Exchange Act of 1934. All broker dealers, investment advisers, and agents are subject to standards of conduct that require the firm and its agents to act in the best interest of retail customers. Regulation BI covers all recommendations to effect securities transactions as well as all recommendations regarding account establishment. That is to say, when recommending that a client open a joint, transfer on death, trust, or fee-based account, the type of account established must be in the client's best interest. In June of 2020, as part of Regulation BI, all broker dealers and investment advisers will be required to provide retail clients with a client relationship summary (CRS) and will be required to post the CRS on their publicly available website. The CRS may be provided in hardcopy or electronically. If the CRS is provided in hardcopy, the CRS may not be more than two pages long and the CRS must be the first page among any documents sent in the same package. The following rules are in place relating to the CRS:

- The CRS must be written in plain English using everyday terms.
- The CRS should be written using "active voice" with a strong, direct, and clear meaning.
- The CRS must follow the standard format and order as detailed by the SEC.
- The CRS should be written as if speaking to the retail investor directly.
- The CRS must be factual and avoid boilerplate, vague, or exaggerated language.
- The CRS may not include disclosures other than those required under Regulation BI.
- Electronic CRSs should use graphs and charts, specifically dual column charts to compare services.
- Electronic CRSs may use videos and popups and must provide access to any referenced information via hyperlink or other means.
- Electronic CRSs may be delivered via email provided that the email contains a direct link to the CRS.

Some of the required disclosures are referred to as "conversation starters." These conversation starters should be in bold or in other text to ensure that they are more noticeable than other disclosures. These conversation starters include questions such as:

1. Who is my primary contact and does he or she represent a broker dealer or an investment adviser?
2. Who can I speak to about how the person is treating me?
3. Given my financial situation, should I choose a brokerage service? Why or why not?
4. Given my financial situation, should I choose an investment advisory service? Why or why not?

5. How will you choose investments to recommend to me?
6. What is your relevant experience, including licenses, education, and qualifications? What do these qualifications mean?
7. What fees will I pay?
8. How will these fees affect my investments? If I give you $10,000, how much will go toward fees and expenses and how much will be invested for me?
9. What are your legal obligations to me when providing recommendations (broker dealer)?
10. What are your legal obligations to me when acting as my investment adviser?
11. How else does your firm make money?
12. How do your financial professionals make money?
13. What conflicts of interest do you have?
14. Does the firm or its financial professionals have legal or disciplinary history?

Both broker dealers and investment advisers are required to adhere to the standards of conduct under Regulation BI. As such, both must disclose that they must put the interests of the client ahead of theirs when making a recommendation and that the way the firm makes money for providing the services causes a conflict of interest. These conflicts include recommending proprietary products, receiving payments from third parties, principal trading, or revenue sharing.

Online broker dealers who only provide access to trading, as well as investment advisers who only offer automated services and who do not offer access to specific registered individuals must disclose this fact in the CRS and must provide a section on their website that answers questions relating to the conversation starters. If a broker dealer or investment adviser provides both online services and access to registered personnel, a registered person must be made available to discuss the conversation starters.

Broker dealers are required to provide the CRS to customers before or upon the earlier of recommending the type of account to establish or investment strategy or upon opening an account or placing an order. Investment advisers must provide the CRS to clients prior to or at the time the contract is entered into even if the contract is oral. The CRS is now known as ADV part 3. For entities who are registered as both a broker dealer and as an investment adviser, the CRS must be delivered upon the earliest requirement for either registration. Any changes required to be made to the CRS must be completed within 30 days and an updated CRS clearly reflecting the changes must be sent to existing customers within 60 days. All broker dealers and investment advisers are required to file the CRS along with any changes with the SEC. Broker dealers will file through the Central Registration Depository (CRD) system and investment advisers will file through the Investment Adviser Registration Database (IARD). The relationship summary must be provided to a client upon request within 30 days.

CHAPTER 2

Definition of Terms

> **INTRODUCTION**
>
> In order to successfully complete the Series 63 exam, it is important to have an in-depth understanding of the terms used within the securities industry—specifically within the framework of the Uniform Securities Act. The terms used by the USA, also known as the Act, may have broader meanings than we are accustomed to in everyday usage.

SECURITY

A security is anything that can be exchanged for value that involves a risk to the holder. A security also represents an investment in an entity managed by a third party. The Howey test was used by the Supreme Court to determine whether something is a security. The test states that a security must meet the following four characteristics:

1. It must be an investment of money.
2. It must involve a common enterprise.
3. It must give the investor an expectation of a profit.
4. It must entail the management of a third party.

The following are examples of securities:

- Stocks
- Bonds

- Notes
- Debentures
- Evidence of indebtedness
- Transferable shares
- Warrants, rights, or options for securities

Most times when you see the term "certificate," you have a security that is a:

- Certificate of interest in profit sharing or a partnership agreement.
- Preorganization certificate.
- Collateral trust certificate.
- Voting trust certificate.
- Certificate of interest in oil or a gas mining title.
- Certificate of deposit for a security, such as an American depositary receipt (ADR) or an American depositary share (ADS).

The term "variable" will also identify a security, as in:

- Variable annuity
- Variable life insurance
- Variable contract

The phrase "interest in" is another key to identifying a security on the Series 63 exam. All of the following are securities:

- Farmland and animals
- Whiskey warehouse receipts
- Commodity options (not futures)
- Insurance company separate accounts
- Real estate condominiums or cooperatives
- Merchandise marketing programs, franchises, or schemes
- Multilevel distributorships, such as Amway

The term "option" is also a good way to identify a security, such as:

- Stock option
- Index option

CHAPTER 2 Definition of Terms

- Futures option
- Commodity futures option

The following are not considered securities:

- Real estate
- Retirement plans, such as IRAs and 401(k)s
- Bank accounts
- Collectibles
- Precious metals
- Fixed annuities/fixed contracts
- Whole and term life policies
- Antiques
- Futures contracts (commodities)
- Trade confirmations
- Prospectuses

The term "future," when it appears alone, is an indication that a security is not involved. However, if the question is asking about a commodity future option or a single stock future, then a security is involved. Also the term "fixed" is a good indication that a security is not involved. If a person commits a fraudulent act in the sale of an investment that is not deemed to be a security, then that person has not violated securities laws but rather has committed a fraudulent act in violation of other state and federal laws.

PERSON

The term "person," as it is used in the USA, refers to any entity that may enter into a legally binding contract. Any entity that can enter into a legally binding contract may transact business in the securities markets. Agreeing to buy or sell a security represents a legally binding contract. For the Series 63, a person is any of the following:

- Natural person
- Corporation
- Trust

- Government organization
- Partnership
- Joint stock company
- Sole proprietor
- Association
- Unincorporated organization

A nonperson is an individual or entity that may not enter into a legally binding contract and therefore may not transact business in the securities market. The following are examples of nonpersons:

- A minor
- Someone deemed to be legally incompetent
- A deceased individual

BROKER DEALER

A broker dealer is a person or a firm that maintains a place of business and affects transactions in the securities markets for its own account or for the account of others. A broker dealer must be registered in its home state as well as in the states of its "individual" clients. A broker dealer is not:

- An agent.
- A bank.
- A savings and loan.
- A person with no place of business in the state, who deals exclusively with financial institutions or issuers.
- A person with no place of business in the state who conducts business with existing clients who do not reside in the state and are in state for less than 30 days.

AGENT

An agent or registered representative may only be an individual (natural person) who represents the issuer or a broker dealer in the purchase and sale or the attempted purchase and sale of securities with the public. Agents are required to register in their home state, their state of employment, and the state of residence of their customers. An agent is not required to register if:

- They represent the issuer or a broker dealer in an underwriting transaction.
- They represent a bank or a savings and loan in the issuance of securities.

Agents who represent exempt issuers are not required to register. Examples of exempt issuers are:

- U.S. government
- State and municipal governments
- Canadian federal and municipal governments
- Commercial paper with maturities of less than 270 days, sold in denominations exceeding $50,000
- Investment contracts associated with employee pension plans, profit sharing, stock purchase, or savings plans
- Foreign national governments recognized by the United States

ISSUER

An issuer is any person that issues or simply proposes to issue a security. Issuers include:

- Corporations.
- U.S. government and agencies.
- State and local governments.

In an issuer or primary transaction, the issuer receives the proceeds from the sale.

NONISSUER

A nonissuer is any entity that does not issue or propose to issue a security. All secondary market transactions that take place on an exchange or in the over-the-counter (OTC) market are nonissuer transactions, and the selling security holder receives the proceeds from the sale.

INVESTMENT ADVISER

An investment adviser is any person who is actively involved in and receives a fee for any of the following:

- Issuing research reports or analysis
- Publishing a market letter based on market events
- Advising clients as to the advisability of the purchase or sale of a security
- Providing investment advisory services as a complement to their services and claiming to provide such services for a fee
- Presenting themselves as investment advisers, also known as the shingle rule
- Pension consultants

PENSION CONSULTANTS

A pension consultant is anyone who advises employees on how to fund their employee benefit plan. A person would also be considered to be a pension consultant if he or she advises the employees on the selection of asset managers or investment advisers for the plan.

An investment adviser is not:

- A bank or savings and loan.
- A broker dealer.
- An agent.
- A lawyer, accountant, teacher, engineer (LATE) whose services are incidental to their business and who do not receive a specific fee for such services.
- Any person exempted by the administrator.
- A federally covered adviser.
- Publishers of newspapers and magazines.

INVESTMENT COUNSEL

The investment Advisers Act of 1940 provides a strict definition as to which professionals may call themselves an investment counsel. An investment counsel must be principally in the business of giving continuous investment advice and must supervise or manage the accounts. The Act does not define how much of the professional's time must be dedicated to providing advice, just that the professional's principal business is giving advice. A key to meeting the definition of an investment counsel are the key words "continuous and regular supervisory or management services." A professional who provides a wide range of services indicates that the professional in question is not principally involved in giving investment advice.

FORM ADV

An investment adviser will begin the formal registration process by filing Form ADV. The ADV form will provide detailed information regarding the investment adviser. The form has four parts: Part 1A, Part 1B, Part 2A, and Part 2B. Form ADV Parts 2A and 2B are provided to clients.

ADV Part 1A provides general information about the investment adviser, including:

- The principal office address.
- Information regarding direct owners.
- Type of organization, such as corporation or partnership.
- How the adviser will conduct business.
- If the firm engages in other activities, such as that of a broker dealer.
- Biographical data on the officers, directors, or partners.
- Disciplinary history of the officers, directors, partners, and the firm.
- Location of books and records if other than principal office.
- If the adviser has custody of customer assets.
- If the adviser has discretionary authority over customer assets.

ADV Part 1B provides details on the indirect owners of the firm and is filed with the state securities administrator for advisers registered at the state level. Advisers who are federally registered do not file ADV Part 1B.

Form ADV part 2A is the adviser's narrative brochure and will disclose information relating to clients. ADV Part 2A will state:

- How and when fees are charged.
- The types of securities the adviser does business in.
- How recommendations are made.
- The type of clients the adviser has.
- The qualifications of officers and directors.

Form ADV Part 2B provides information relating to individuals who:

- Provide investment advice and who have direct contact with advisory clients.
- Have discretion over client assets, regardless of whether the individual has contact with clients.

New rules have been enacted to further enhance the required disclosures by investment advisers. These enhanced disclosures are designed to provide more information to both clients and regulators regarding the adviser's business. Investment advisers must now also disclose the following on form ADV:

- The total number of offices and detailed information relating to the adviser's 25 largest offices.
- Detailed information regarding the adviser's separately managed account including the type of assets held, the use of derivatives, leverage and ownership or operation of private funds.
- Detailed information regarding the number of clients serviced by the adviser and amount of assets managed for each category of client i.e. individual, institutional etc.
- Advisers with over $1 billion in assets under management must report the value of their AUM within one of three ranges $1–10 billion, $10–50 billion and greater than $50 billion.
- Advisers who utilize social media must disclose all social media accounts such as Facebook, Twitter, LinkedIn and all websites operated for the adviser's business
- If the chief compliance officer of the firm is employed at any other adviser the fact must be disclosed to but not approved by regulators.

INVESTMENT ADVISER REGISTRATION DATABASE (IARD)

Investment Advisers will file Form ADV and all of the required parts based on their business profile and place of registration through the Investment Adviser Registration Database or IARD. The IARD is a centralized clearinghouse for all investment adviser registrations. Advisers electronically file all required registration documents, disclosures, and any required updates or amendments through the IARD. The IARD is used by the SEC and NASAA to review all investment adviser registration data. Advisers must file annual updates to their Form ADV within 90 days of the end of the adviser's fiscal year. It is at this time that the adviser will certify the value of the assets under the adviser's control. Advisers most promptly file any changes to the adviser's business and to Form ADV through the IARD. These changes include any:

- Change of the business location.
- Name changes.

- Changes in custody policy or location of assets.
- Material changes to the adviser's brochure.
- Change of contact information or personnel.
- Change in legal structure (how the firm is organized i.e., corporation partnership, etc.).
- Changes to disciplinary history.
- Change in location of books and records.

INVESTMENT ADVISER REPRESENTATIVE

An investment adviser representative is a natural person who is under the control of the investment adviser and includes:

- Officers and directors.
- Partners.
- Solicitors.
- Supervisors.

Clerical employees are not considered investment advisory representatives and are not required to register.

SOLICITOR

A solicitor is any person who for compensation actively seeks new business for an investment adviser. A solicitor can also include professionals who refer clients to the investment adviser for a fee. All solicitors must be registered as investment adviser representatives. Investors who are introduced to an adviser through the use of a solicitor must be provided with the solicitor's brochure. The solicitor's brochure will provide the client of the details of the solicitor's relationship with the adviser and the compensation arrangement including the amount of the management fee paid to the solicitor. If the client is paying a higher fee by being introduced to the adviser by the solicitor, that fact must be disclosed as well. The solicitor's professional background is not required to be disclosed in the brochure.

ACCESS PERSON

An access person is anyone employed by the investment adviser who has access to nonpublic information relating to activity and holding in client accounts or in the investment adviser's portfolio account. A person will also be deemed to be an access person if that individual makes recommendations to clients or has access to recommendations prior to the release of such recommendations. All of the firms officers and directors are deemed to be access persons at advisory firms where the primary business is providing investment advice. All access persons must report their personal transactions to the firm's chief compliance officer or duly designated compliance officer. The firm must maintain a list of all individuals who were deemed to be access persons in the last five years.

INSTITUTIONAL INVESTOR

An institutional investor is a person or firm who trades securities for his or her own account or for the account of others. Institutional investors are generally limited to large financial companies. Because of their size and sophistication, fewer protective laws cover institutional investors. It is important to note that there is no minimum size for an institutional account. Institutional investors include:

- Broker dealers.
- Investment advisers.
- Investment companies.
- Insurance companies.
- Banks.
- Trusts.
- Savings and loans.
- Government agencies.
- Employment benefit plans with more than $1,000,000 in assets.

ACCREDITED INVESTOR

An accredited investor is an individual who meets one or more of the following criteria:

- Has a net worth of $1,000,000, excluding the primary residence

or

- Earns $200,000 per year or more for the last two years and has the expectation of earning the same in the current year

  or

- Is part of a couple earning $300,000 per year or more

The SEC has recently added a new category that will allow an individual to qualify as an accredited investor. Individuals who meet certain educational or certification requirements can now meet the definition of accredited investor. Included in this category are individuals who have an active Series 7, 65 or 82 license.

QUALIFIED PURCHASER

A qualified purchaser must meet strict minimum financial requirements. Securities sold to qualified purchasers are not required to register in the state where the qualified purchaser resides. A qualified purchaser is:

- An individual with at least $5,000,000 in investments.
- A family-owned business with at least $5,000,000 in investments.
- A trust sponsored by qualified purchasers.

PRIVATE INVESTMENT COMPANY

A private investment company is an unregistered investment company or hedge fund that raises funds through the sale of securities to qualified purchasers for any business purposes.

OFFER/OFFER TO SELL/OFFER TO BUY

An offer is any attempt to solicit the purchase or sale of a security for value. An offer is considered to have been made in the state where the offer originated, as well as in the state where it is received or directed. An offer will not be considered to have been made if it was received through a television or radio broadcast originating outside the state. Additionally, an offer will not be considered to have been made if received by a newspaper or magazine published out of the state or by a magazine published in state that has two-thirds of its paid circulation outside of the state. The state securities administrator does not have jurisdiction over offers that are deemed to be made exclusively outside of the administrator's state.

SALE/SELL

To sell a security, its ownership must be conveyed for value. A sale is considered to have been made at the time of the contract (trade). A sale of a security that has warrants or a right attached is also considered a sale of the attached security. A sale of any security that is convertible or exercisable into another security is considered to include a sale of the security for which the security is convertible or exercisable. A gift of assessable stock is also considered to be a sale. Assessable stock is stock that may require the holder to make additional payments as a term of ownership. A sale does not include a dividend or the pledge of a security for a collateral loan.

GUARANTEE/GUARANTEED

The term "guarantee" means that another party other than the issuer of the security has guaranteed the payment of principal, interest, or dividends. Only three parties may guarantee something. They are:

1. U.S. government
2. Insurance company
3. Parent company (they may guarantee obligations of a subsidiary)

12B-1 FEES

Most mutual funds charge an asset-based distribution fee to cover expenses related to the promotion and distribution of the fund's shares. The amount of the fee will be determined annually as a percentage of the NAV or as a flat fee. The 12B-1 fee will be charged to the shares quarterly, reducing the investor's overall return on the fund. Because a 12B-1 fee reduces the return, it is a type of sales load. 12B-1 fees cover such things as the printing of prospectuses and certain sales commissions to agents. To start and continue a

12B-1 fee, three votes must initially approve the fee and annually reapprove it. The three votes that are required are:

- A majority vote of the board of directors.
- A majority vote of the noninterested board of directors.
- A majority vote of the outstanding shares.

To terminate a 12B-1 fee, only two votes are required. They are:

- A majority vote of the noninterested board of directors.
- A majority vote of the outstanding shares.

LIMITS OF A 12B-1 FEE

A mutual fund that distributes its own shares and markets itself as a no-load fund may charge a 12B-1 fee that is no more than .25%. If the fund charges a 12B-1 fee that is greater than .25%, it may not be called a no-load fund. Other funds that do not call themselves a no-load fund are limited to .75% of assets, and the amount of the 12B-1 fee must be reasonably related to the anticipated level of expenses incurred for promotion and distribution. All 12B-1 fees are reviewed quarterly.

CONTUMACY

Contumacy is the willful display of contempt for the administrator's order. An act of contumacy may result in the agent's or firm's registration being revoked or other disciplinary action. The administrator may petition the court to have a person who has displayed contumacy for their order to be found in contempt of court. A finding of contempt of court may result in the court ordering a jail term.

FEDERALLY COVERED EXEMPTION

A federally covered exemption provides for a full exemption from state registration for federally covered investment advisers and federally covered securities.

A federally covered investment adviser is one that meets the requirements for assets under management and is registered with the Securities and Exchange Commission (SEC).

A federally covered security is any of the following:

- A security listed on a centralized U.S. stock exchange or on the Nasdaq
- An investment company security issued under the Investment Company Act of 1940
- Securities sold to qualified purchasers
- Securities with information available in a nationally recognized manual, such as Moody's or S&P

POWER OF ATTORNEY

A power of attorney once given to an individual allows that person to make decisions on behalf of the grantor with the same force and effect as if the grantor himself had entered into the agreement. Most powers of attorney in the investment world are limited powers of attorney that allow an investment professional to purchase and sell securities without speaking to a client first. A full power of attorney will allow the individual to withdrawal cash and securities from an account. A standard power of attorney will terminate upon the death or incapacitation of the grantor. A durable power of attorney will remain in full force during the incapacitation of the grantor and will only terminate upon the grantor's death. Discretion may not be exercised until the power of attorney has been received and approved.

ESCHEATMENT

In the event an account owner cannot be located after a significant effort by the broker dealer or investment adviser, the account will be considered to be abandoned and the state will claim the account through the escheatment process. The state will hold the account on its records as a bookkeeping entry. The former account owner or their estate may make a claim for the assets if they become aware of the existence of the account. The amount of time that must pass prior to an asset being deemed abandoned and being turned over to the state varies between asset classes and from state to state.

CHAPTER 2

Pretest

DEFINITION OF TERMS

1. Which of the following is NOT considered a person under the Uniform Securities Act (USA)?
   a. A joint stock company
   b. A trust
   c. A 17-year-old honor student
   d. A government agency

2. Which of the following is NOT considered a sale of a security?
   a. A gift of assessable stock
   b. A contract to convey ownership for value
   c. A pledge of securities as collateral for a margin loan
   d. A bonus of securities

3. Which of the following is the minimum financial requirement for an individual to be considered a qualified purchaser?
   a. $1,000,000
   b. $2,500,000
   c. $5,000,000 individually or $10,000,000 jointly with a spouse
   d. $5,000,000 individually or jointly with a spouse

4. As it pertains to the USA, which of the following are considered institutional investors?
    I. A bank
    II. An insurance company
    III. An employee benefit plan with $800,000 in assets
    IV. A trust
    a. I and II
    b. I and IV
    c. I, II, and IV
    d. I, II, III, and IV

5. All of the following are considered securities, EXCEPT:
    a. whiskey warehouse receipts.
    b. a trust indenture.
    c. a commodity future option.
    d. interest in a marketing scheme.

6. An individual gives 1,500 shares of assessable stock to his child. Under the USA this is:
    a. subject to approval of the state securities administrator.
    b. considered an offer of securities.
    c. irrevocable.
    d. considered a sale of securities.

7. Which of the following is considered an investment adviser?
    a. The publisher of a market report with a $495 subscription fee based on market events
    b. A publisher of a financial newspaper
    c. An accountant
    d. A person paid a commission for executing a securities transaction

CHAPTER 2 Pretest

8. Which of the following is considered a qualified purchaser?
   a. An individual with $1,000,000 in investments held jointly with a spouse and with annual income of $375,000
   b. A publicly held company with at least $5,000,000 in net assets
   c. A pension plan with $2,000,000 in assets
   d. A family-owned business with at least $5,000,000 in assets

9. XYZ common stock trades on the Boston Stock Exchange. XYZ common stock is an example of a(n):
   a. blue-chip security.
   b. federally covered security.
   c. exempt security.
   d. security of an exempt issuer.

10. A security is represented by an interest in which of the following?
    I. Farmland or animals
    II. A cooperative
    III. A marketing scheme
    IV. A multilevel distributorship
    a. None of these
    b. I and II
    c. I, II, and III
    d. I, II, III, and IV

11. Under the USA, which of the following are considered to be an investment adviser?
    I. XYZ Advisers, Inc.
    II. Mr. Jones, the owner of XYZ Advisers, Inc.
    III. The publisher of a market-based letter charging $800 per year
    IV. A partner for XYZ who solicits new clients for XYZ Advisers, Inc.
    a. I only
    b. I and III
    c. I, II, and IV
    d. I, II, III, and IV

12. When using the Howey test to determine if an investment is a security, all of the following are used, EXCEPT:
    a. third-party management.
    b. investment of money.
    c. a common enterprise.
    d. the promise of a profit.

13. A broker is a(n):
    a. registered representative.
    b. duly licensed agent.
    c. issuer of collateralized securities.
    d. person who executes transactions for the accounts of others.

14. An offer of securities is considered to have been made in which of the following circumstances?
    a. A sales presentation for a fixed annuity
    b. Delivering a market report
    c. Mailing a form letter
    d. Delivering a prospectus

15. The Uniform Securities Act defines an issuer as a:
    a. broker dealer.
    b. bank.
    c. corporation proposing the sale of common shares.
    d. savings and loan.

16. An individual in which of the following situations is considered an agent?
    a. An individual who represents a bank as the issuer of securities
    b. An individual who represents a corporate issuer in the sale of large-denomination commercial paper
    c. An individual who represents a Canadian province
    d. An individual who represents an out-of-state broker dealer selling securities to residents

CHAPTER 2   Pretest

17. Which of the following is NOT a broker dealer?
    I. A firm with no office in the state that transacts business only with existing customers who do not reside within the state
    II. A firm with no office in the state that transacts business only with broker dealers in the state
    III. A firm with an office in the state that only transacts business with other broker dealers
    IV. A firm with no office in the state that only transacts business with wealthy clients in the state
    a. I and II
    b. II and IV
    c. I, II, and IV
    d. I, II, III, and IV

18. Which of the following is NOT a federally covered security?
    a. A security issued by an investment company
    b. A security issued by a UIT
    c. A security only sold to qualified purchasers
    d. A security listed on Nasdaq OTCBB

19. A guarantee may be issued by which of the following?
    I. An insurance company
    II. The U.S. government
    III. A parent company
    IV. An investment adviser
    a. I and IV
    b. I and III
    c. I, II, and III
    d. I, II, III, and IV

20. An offer to sell has been made:
   a. when stock has been pledged as collateral for a loan at the bank.
   b. when a gift of securities to a charity results in tax credit for the donor.
   c. when a representative calls a client and recommends a security.
   d. when an account is transferred to the surviving party under joint tenants with rights of survivorship.

CHAPTER 3

Registration of Broker Dealers, Investment Advisers, and Agents

INTRODUCTION

In this chapter we will examine the state registration process for broker dealers, investment advisers, and agents. An important part of this chapter will be to know when registration is required and when an exemption is offered to the subject in question.

REGISTRATION OF BROKER DEALERS AND AGENTS

Prior to conducting business in any state, a broker dealer must be properly registered or exempt from registration in that state. The first test when deciding if the broker dealer must register is determining if the firm has an office in the state. If the firm maintains an office within the state, then it must register with that state. Agents must register in their state of residence even if their firm is located in another state.

EXAMPLE An agent who lives in New Jersey and who commutes to an office in New York must register in both New Jersey and New York.

Agents must also register in the states where they sell securities or offer to sell securities as well as where they advertise. If the firm does not have an office in the state it may or may not be required to register, depending on whom it does business with. If a broker dealer does not have an office in the state and engages in securities transactions with the general public, then it must register. If a broker dealer with no office in the state conducts business exclusively with any of the following, it is not required to register in that state:

- Other broker dealers
- Issuers of securities
- Investment companies
- Insurance companies
- Banks
- Savings and loans
- Trust companies
- Pension plans with more than $1,000,000 in assets
- Other financial institutions
- Institutional buyers
- Existing customers with less than 30 days temporary residency in the state (on vacation or business trips)

A broker dealer will not be deemed to have a place of business in a state where it does not maintain an office simply by virtue of the fact that the firm's website is accessible from that state so long as the following conditions are met:

- The firm's website clearly states that the firm may only conduct business in states where it is properly registered to do so.
- The firm's website only provides general information about the firm and does not provide specific investment advice.
- The firm may not respond to Internet inquiries with the intent to solicit business without first meeting the registration requirements in the state of the prospective customer.

AGENT REGISTRATION

It is unlawful for a broker dealer to employ any agent who is not properly registered under the Uniform Securities Act (USA). When determining if an agent must register, you must first look at whom the agent works for. If the agent works for a broker dealer, the agent must register. The only exception is for officers and directors of a broker dealer who have no involvement with customers, securities transactions, or supervision. If the agent works for an exempt issuer, the agent is exempt from registration no matter what security is involved. Exempt issuers are:

- U.S. and municipal governments.
- Canadian federal and municipal governments.
- Foreign federal governments recognized by the United States.
- Banks, savings and loans, and trust companies.

Agents are also exempt from registering if they represent an issuer in the sale of an exempt security, such as:

- Bankers' acceptances or time drafts with less than 270 days to maturity sold in denominations of $50,000 or more.
- Investment contracts relating to employee savings, stock purchases, pension plans, or other benefit plans, as long as no commission is received for such sales.

REGISTERING BROKER DEALERS

A broker dealer wishing to become registered in a state must first file an application with the state securities administrator. The broker dealer must also pay all filing fees and sign consent to service of process. By signing the consent to service of process, the broker dealer appoints the administrator as its attorney in fact and allows the administrator to receive legal papers for the applicant. Any legal papers received by the administrator will have the same force and effect as if they were served on the broker dealer. All applications must also include:

- Type of organization (corporation, partnership)
- Address of business
- Description of business to be conducted
- Backgrounds and qualifications of officers and directors
- Disclosure of any legal actions
- Financial condition

The firm's registration will become effective at noon 30 days after the initial application has been received or at noon 30 days after the administrator has received the last piece of required information. Registering a broker dealer in a state automatically requires that any officers and directors who act in a sales capacity register as agents in that state.

TAKENOTE!

Broker dealers must always register with the SEC and with states where they conduct business.

FINANCIAL REQUIREMENTS

A broker dealer must be able to meet the minimum capital requirements set forth by the state securities administrator. If the broker dealer is unable to meet this capital requirement, it must post a surety bond to ensure its solvency. Broker dealers that meet the SEC minimum net capital requirements are exempt from USA's capital and surety bond requirements. The amount of the bond required by the administrator for broker dealers who have custody or discretion over client accounts is limited to the amount of capital required by the Securities Exchange Act of 1934. No bond may be required of broker dealers whose capital exceeds the amount of the bond required by the administrator. The administrator may require that an officer or agent of the broker dealer take an exam that may be oral, written, or both.

TAKENOTE!

No state or political subdivision may enact a requirement for registration that requires a broker dealer to meet a financial, record keeping, reporting, or custody requirement that goes beyond that required by The Securities Exchange Act of 1934.

BROKER DEALERS ON THE PREMISES OF OTHER FINANCIAL INSTITUTIONS

As the financial services business continues to bring together investment services with other more traditional banking services, it is more common to see brokerage services offered at retail bank locations. Broker dealers who offer investment services at bank branches must follow certain guidelines. The setting in which the broker dealer conducts its business should be separate from where the retail banking business is being conducted, if practical. Broker dealers must disclose to the customer, at or before the time that the customer opens the account, that the deposits are not guaranteed by the FDIC or the financial institution and are subject to the loss of principal. These same disclosures must also appear in all advertising and sales literature issued by the broker dealer operating on the location of other financial institutions. The host financial institution must sign an agreement stating that FINRA and the SEC are allowed to have access to any location where the member conducts its business. The member is required to promptly notify the financial institution if it terminates an associated person for cause.

HIRING NEW EMPLOYEES

A registered principal of a firm will be the individual who interviews and screens potential new employees. The principal will be required to make a thorough investigation into the candidate's professional and personal backgrounds. With few exceptions, other than clerical personnel, all new employees will be required to become registered as an associated person with the firm. The new employee will begin the registration process by filling out and submitting a Uniform Application for Securities Industry Registration, also known as Form U4. Form U4 is used to collect the applicant's personal and professional history, including:

- 10-year employment history
- 5-year resident history
- Legal name and any aliases used
- Any legal or regulatory actions

The principal of the firm is required to verify the employment information for the last 3 years and must attest to the character of the applicant by signing Form U4 prior to its submission to FINRA. All U4 forms will be sent to the Central Registration Depository (CRD) along with a fingerprint card for processing and recording. The employing firm must maintain written procedures to verify the accuracy of the information on the new hire's U4 form. A comprehensive review of the information must take place within 30 days of the form being submitted to FINRA. Fingerprint cards may be submitted in hard copy or electronically. The candidate's fingerprints will be submitted to the FBI for review. If after 3 good faith attempts to submit fingerprints the FBI determines that the fingerprints are ineligible or cannot be read the candidate will not be asked to submit a fourth set of fingerprints and the FBI will conduct a name check to search the candidate's history. Any applicant who has answered yes to any of the questions on the form regarding his or her background must give a detailed explanation in the DRP pages attached to the form. The applicant is not required to provide information regarding:

- Marital status
- Educational background
- Income or net worth

Information regarding the employee's finances is disclosed on Form U4 if the associated person has ever declared bankruptcy and if the employee has any unsatisfied judgements or liens. Any development that would cause an answer on the associated person's U4 to change requires that the member update the U4 within 30 days of when the member becomes informed of the event. In the case of an event that could cause the individual to become statutorily disqualified, such as a felony conviction or misdemeanor involving cash or securities, the member must update the associated person's U4 within 10 business days of learning of the event. Additionally, broker dealers are required to perform background checks on its employees every 5 years to ensure that no judgements, liens or disclosable events have gone unreported by the registered person. Registered persons who fail to disclose an unsatisfied judgements or liens are subject to significant regulatory action that could result in the person being barred from the industry in extreme cases.

RESIGNATION OF A REGISTERED REPRESENTATIVE

If a registered representative voluntarily resigns or has his or her association with a member firm terminated for any reason, the member must fill out and submit a Uniform Termination Notice for Securities Industry Registration, which is known as Form U5. The member must submit the form to FINRA within 30 days of the termination. The member firm is also required to give a copy of the form to the representative upon termination. The member must also state the reason for the termination, either voluntary or for cause. Voluntary terminations cover all terminations that were not the result of the agent being fired for violations of industry or company regulations, such as staff reductions. An associated person's registration is nontransferable. A representative may not simply move his or her registration from one firm to another. The employing firm that the representative is leaving must fill out and submit a Form U5 to FINRA, which terminates the representative's registration. The new employing firm must fill out and submit a new Form U4 to begin a new registration for the associated person with the new employer. The new employer is required to obtain a copy of the U5 form filed by the old employing member either from the employee or directly from FINRA within 60 days of submitting the new U4. The previous employer is not required to provide a copy to the new member firm. If the new employing member asks the associated person for a copy of the U5, the member has two business days to provide it. If the member requests a copy of the U5 from the agent who has not received a copy of his or her U5 from the old employer, the agent must promptly request it from the old employer and provide it to the new employer within 2 business days of receipt. Should an agent's previous employer discover facts that would alter the information on Form U5, the previous employer must file an amended Form U5 within 30 days and provide a copy to the former employee. A representative who leaves the industry for more than 24 months is required to requalify by exam. During a period of absence from the industry of 2 years or less, FINRA retains jurisdiction over the representative in cases involving customer complaints and violations.

TAKENOTE!

A firm may not allow an inactive agent to "park" his or her license with the firm and may not maintain an inactive agent's license on the books simply to ensure that the agent does not have to requalify by exam. The one exception to the rule is for agents in the military who are called to active duty. While on active duty, the agent's registration and continuing education requirements will be "tolled" until he or she returns. While on active duty the agent may not conduct business but may receive commissions generated from his or her book of business. Once the agent returns from active duty he or she has 90 days to reenter the securities industry. If after 90 days the agent does not reenter the business, the 24-month window begins.

MAINTAINING QUALIFICATIONS PROGRAM

FINRA has implemented a continuing education program designed to allow eligible agents and principals to maintain their qualifications for up to 5 years from the date of termination. It is important to note that this program does not eliminate the 24 month window. It provides terminated individuals with the option to maintain their licenses during extended absences from the industry. Through the maintaining qualifications program or MQP, eligible persons who leave to start families or to pursue other interests will be allowed to reenter the industry without being required to requalify by exam. It also allows active agents who have one or more of their registrations terminated through filing of a a partial U5 to maintain the terminated registration. To be eligible to participate individuals must:

- Have been registered in the terminated category for at least 1 year prior to the termination
- Elect to participate in MQP within 2 years of terminating the registration
- Complete all CE requirements by their assigned due date

Individuals who have been inactive for more than 2 years or who have been or who subsequently become statutorily disqualified will be deemed ineligible. The MQP requires individuals to complete annual CE courses containing both regulatory and practical element training and to pay annual fees to participate. Participants in the MQP program will access the courses through the FinPro system.

REGISTERING AGENTS

Most states require that agents successfully complete the Series 63 exam before they may conduct business within their state. In addition to successfully passing the Series 63, agents must also:

- Abide by and understand state securities laws and regulations.
- Recognize that the state may require additional certification regarding the state's securities laws.
- Understand that they may not conduct business until they are properly registered.

While an agent's registration is pending the agent may act in an administrative or support capacity only. The agent may assist with the preparation of research, trade input, and other support functions but may not act in any capacity of an agent.

CHAPTER 3 Registration of Broker Dealers, Investment Advisers, and Agents

> **TESTFOCUS!**
>
> - An agent does not become registered in a state simply by passing the Series 63 exam. An agent becomes registered only when the state securities administrator notifies the agent that he or she has become registered.
> - An agent may not be registered in any state without being employed by a broker dealer or issuer, and no broker dealer or issuer shall employ an agent who is not duly registered.

CHANGES IN AN AGENT'S EMPLOYMENT

When an agent changes firms, the agent, former employer, and new employer all must notify the state securities administrator. This is done in most cases quite easily through the Central Registration Depository (CRD) system for all firm and agent information. An agent's termination becomes effective 30 days after notifying the state unless the administrator is in the process of suspending or revoking the agent's registration. The administrator may still revoke an agent's registration for up to one year after the registration has been terminated. If an agent is denied a registration as the result of information received on the agent's form U5 termination notice filed by the agent's previous employer, only the new employer and the agent will be notified of the denial.

MERGERS AND ACQUISITIONS OF FIRMS

If a broker dealer is acquiring another broker dealer, the successor firm must file an application for registration within the state. The successor firm's registration will become effective upon completion of the transaction. The registration fees for the successor firm will be waived.

RENEWING REGISTRATIONS

All state registrations expire on December 31, and all broker dealers, investment advisers, and agents are required to file a renewal application and pay a renewal fee. The consent to service of process does not get refiled with the renewal applications. The consent to service of process remains in effect as long as the registration of the agent or firm is in effect with the state.

CANADIAN FIRMS AND AGENTS

A Canadian firm or agent may engage in securities transactions with financial institutions and existing customers without registering under the USA as long as they do not maintain an office within the state. A Canadian broker dealer or agent who is a member in good standing with a Canadian securities regulator is allowed to register through a simplified registration process. The state registration will become effective 30 days after the application has been received with the consent to service process. The Canadian broker dealer must advise the state of any disciplinary action.

INVESTMENT ADVISER REGISTRATION

It is unlawful for an investment adviser to conduct securities business without being properly registered or exempt from registration. State registration exemptions are provided for investment advisers who:

- Are federally registered.
- Manage portfolios for investment companies.
- Manage portfolios in excess of $110,000,000.
- Have no office in the state and conduct business exclusively with financial institutions.
- Have no office in the state and offer advice to five clients or fewer in any 12-month period. This is known as the de minimis exemption.

If a state registered investment adviser with no office in the state advertises to the public the ability to meet and offer investment advisory services with clients in a hotel or other temporary location, the investment adviser is required to register with the state.

An investment adviser will not be deemed to have a place of business in a state where it does not maintain an office simply by virtue of the fact that the firm's website is accessible from that state so long as the following conditions are met:

- The firm's website clearly states that the firm may only conduct business in states where it is properly registered to do so.
- The firm's website only provides general information about the firm and does not provide specific investment advice.

- The firm may not respond to Internet inquiries with the intent to solicit business without first meeting the registration requirements in the state of the prospective customer.

THE NATIONAL SECURITIES MARKET IMPROVEMENT ACT OF 1996/THE COORDINATION ACT

The National Securities Markets Improvement Act of 1996 eliminated regulatory duplication of effort and established registration requirements for investment advisers. A federally covered investment adviser must register with the SEC and is any investment adviser who:

- Manages at least $110,000,000.
- Manages investment company portfolios.
- Is not registered under state laws.

All federally registered investment advisers must pay state filing fees and notify the administrator in the states in which they conduct business. The state securities administrator may not audit a federally covered investment adviser unless that adviser's principal office is located in that administrator's state. Investment advisers are required to register with the state if they manage less than $100,000,000. Once the investment adviser reaches $100,000,000 in assets under management (AUM), the adviser becomes eligible for federal registration. An investment adviser who manages between $100,000,000 and $110,000,000 may choose to register either with the state or with the SEC. Investment advisers who think that their asset base will exceed $110,000,000 should register with the SEC within 90 days of reaching $110,000,000 in AUM. An adviser applying for federal registration with SEC will file Form ADV and the adviser's registration will become effective within 45 days. Investment advisers who manage $110,000,000 or more must register with the SEC. If a federally covered investment adviser's AUM falls below $90,000,000, the adviser must withdraw its federal registration by filling form ADV-W within 60 days and must be registered with the appropriate states within 180 days. Like most regulations, there are rare exceptions to the rule of when an investment adviser may register with the SEC. The Dodd-Frank Wall Street Reform Act of 2010 increased the AUM for federal registration to its current levels and defined three categories of investment advisers, as follows:

1. Small adviser: Advisers with less than $25,000,000 AUM

2. Midsize advisers: Advisers with $25,000,000 to $100,000,000 AUM
3. Large advisers: Advisers with more than $100,000,000 AUM

Pension consultants must have at least $200,000,000 AUM to be eligible to become federally registered.

INVESTMENT ADVISER REPRESENTATIVE

All investment adviser representatives who maintain an office within the state must register within the state. An investment adviser representative is an individual who:

- Gives advice on the value of the securities.
- Gives advice on the advisability of buying or selling securities.
- Solicits new advisory clients.
- Is an officer, director, or partner of the investment adviser.

An investment adviser may not employ any representative who is not properly registered. Clerical and administrative employees are not considered representatives and do not need to register. An investment adviser representative who has no place of business in the state and who offers to meet a client in a hotel or other place of convenience is not considered to have an office in the state so long as the representative does not advertise the office and only offers the ability to meet directly to clients.

TESTFOCUS!

Investment adviser representatives who represent federally covered investment advisers are only required to register in the state where they work even though they may have clients in other states, and the federally covered adviser is not required to register.

INVESTMENT ADVISER REGISTRATION

An investment advisory firm that is required to register with the state must file the following with the state securities administrator before it becomes registered:

- Application Form ADV
- Filing fees
- Audited balance sheet within 90 days of year end
- Consent to service of process

CAPITAL REQUIREMENTS

State registered investment advisers must maintain a minimal level of financial solvency. Advisers that have custody of customers' cash and securities must maintain minimum net capital of $35,000. Advisers that are unable to meet this requirement may post a surety bond. Deposits of cash and securities will alleviate the surety bond requirement. Advisers are considered to have custody if they have their customers' cash and securities held at their firm or if they have full discretion over their customers' accounts. Full discretion allows the adviser to withdraw cash and securities from customers' accounts without consulting the customer. Advisers who have only limited discretionary authority over customers' accounts need to maintain a minimum of $10,000 in net capital. Advisers with limited discretionary authority may only buy and sell securities for a customer's benefit without consulting the customer; the adviser may not withdraw or deposit cash or securities without the customer's consent. If a state registered investment adviser meets the capital requirements in its home state, it will be deemed to have met the capital requirements in any other state in which the adviser wishes to register, even if the other states have higher net capital or bonding requirements. Should a state registered adviser's net capital fall below the minimum requirement, the adviser must notify the state administrator by the close of the next business day of the adviser's net worth. The adviser must then file a financial disclosure report with the administrator by the end of the next business day. If the adviser has fallen below the net worth requirement the adviser will be required to post a bond to cover any capital deficiency. The amount of the bond will be rounded up to the nearest $5,000. Investment advisers with custody of funds must maintain a positive net worth at all times. Investment adviser representatives are not required to maintain a minimum level of liquidity. Federally registered investment advisers are not required to meet any capital or net worth requirements.

EXAMS

The state securities administrator may require investment adviser representatives, as well as the officers and directors of the firm, to take an exam, which may be oral, written, or both. All registrations become effective at noon 30 days after the application has been filed or at noon 30 days after the last piece of information is received by the administrator. The administrator may require that an announcement of the investment adviser's intended registration be published in the newspaper.

Requirement	Broker Dealer	Investment Adviser	Agents
Net capital	Yes	Yes	No
Surety bond	Yes	Yes	Yes
Exams	Yes	Yes	Yes
Fees	Yes	Yes	Yes

 TAKENOTE!

In practice the administrator may allow registrations of any applicant to become effective in a period of less than 30 days. This would be classified by definition as a "rush order." During the period when an agent's registration is pending the person may not undertake any activities that would require the person to be registered. The person may only act in a clerical capacity such as posting trades to client accounts and participating in the creation of research.

ADVERTISING AND SALES LITERATURE

All advertising and sales literature for an investment adviser must be filed with the state securities administrator. The administrator may require prior approval of:

- Form letters
- Prospectuses
- Pamphlets

CHAPTER 3 Registration of Broker Dealers, Investment Advisers, and Agents

The following records must be kept by investment advisers for a minimum of five years unless the state securities administrator requires a different period of time:

- Advertising and sales literature
- Account statements
- Order tickets/order memorandum

All investment advisers must keep accurate records relating to the following:

- Cash receipts and disbursements
- Income and expense ledgers
- Order tickets, including customer's name
- Adviser's name, including executing broker and discretionary information
- Ledgers and confirmations for all customers for whom the adviser has custody
- Financial statements and trial balance
- All written recommendations to customers
- Copies of advertisements, circulars, and articles sent to more than 10 people (NASAA requires copies of records sent to 2 or more people to be maintained.)
- Copies of calculations sent to more than 10 people (NASAA requires copies of records sent to 2 or more people to be maintained.)

All books and records must be kept for five years readily accessible and for two years at the adviser's office. Records may be kept on a computer or microfiche as long as the data may be viewed and printed.

BROCHURE DELIVERY

An investment adviser is required to provide all prospective clients with a brochure or with Form ADV Part 2A and 2B at least 48 hours prior to the signing of the contract or at least at the time of the signing of the contract, if the client is given a five-day grace period to withdraw without penalty. The brochure or Form ADV Part 2 will state:

- How and when fees are charged.
- The types of securities the adviser does business in.
- How recommendations are made.
- The type of clients the adviser has.
- The qualifications of officers and directors.

The NASAA Model Rule regarding direct fee deduction from client accounts, by advisers who use a qualified custodian, requires advisers who automatically deduct fees to have the written authorization from each client to deduct the fees directly from client accounts. An invoice must be sent to the clients detailing the fee as well as the formula for determining the fee. If the fee is based on the value of the account the value of the account at the time the fee is charged must be provided. The statements for client accounts will be sent by the qualified custodian not from the investment adviser. NASAA considers a qualified custodian to be any of the following three entities:

1. A banking institution covered by FDIC insurance
2. A registered broker dealer in the business of holding or carrying customer funds and securities
3. A foreign financial institution in the business of providing such services who segregates' customer assets from its own

WRAP ACCOUNTS

A wrap account is an account that charges one fee for both the advice received as well as the cost of the transaction. All clients who open wrap accounts must be given the wrap account brochure knows as schedule H, which will provide all of the information that is found on Form ADV Part 2. Broker dealers who offer WRAP accounts must be registered as investment advisers. Individuals who receive fee based compensation generated by WRAP fee programs must be registered as investment adviser representatives.

CHAPTER 3

Pretest

REGISTRATION OF BROKER DEALERS, INVESTMENT ADVISERS, AND AGENTS

1. An individual representing which of the following is always required to register?
   a. Government
   b. Nonexempt issuers
   c. Issuers in the sale of commercial paper
   d. A broker dealer

2. A broker dealer is exempt from the surety bond requirement if the broker dealer:
   a. does not maintain an office in the state.
   b. deals only with existing customers.
   c. meets the SEC's net capital requirement.
   d. has customer funds segregated from its own funds.

3. An investment adviser may conduct business with how many people and still qualify for the de minimis exemption?
   a. Fewer than 12 in 6 months
   b. Fewer than 10 in 12 months
   c. Fewer than 5 in 12 months
   d. Fewer than 8 in 12 months

4. A small New Jersey broker dealer with five partners who all manage client portfolios registers as a broker dealer in Connecticut. Which of the following is true?
   a. Only the partners with clients in Connecticut must register as agents in the state.
   b. Only one of the partners is required to register as a supervisor for all of the firm's activities in Connecticut.
   c. There is no requirement for the partners of a broker dealer to register in a state where the firm has no office.
   d. All of the partners must register.

5. All of the following give investment advice that is related to their business. Which of the following must register as an investment adviser?
   a. A teacher giving advice on a 403B plan
   b. An engineer giving advice on the feasibility of a bridge
   c. A pension consultant overseeing pensions with $300,000,000 in assets
   d. An accountant giving advice on municipal bonds

6. You work for a newly formed investment adviser that has just received $107,000,000 to manage. The firm should register with which of the following?
   a. With the SEC only
   b. With the state only
   c. With either the SEC or the state, depending on the prospects for receiving additional funds
   d. The adviser does not have to register if it has no office in the state

7. Which of the following does NOT have to be disclosed to a new investment advisory client?
   a. Type of clients
   b. Basis for recommendations
   c. Advisory fees
   d. Investment adviser representative's compensation

8. An agent is exempt from registration if she represents which of the following?
    I. A municipality
    II. A Canadian corporation
    III. A trust company
    IV. The government of Brazil
    a. I and IV
    b. I and II
    c. I, III, and IV
    d. I, II, III, and IV

9. Which of the following must withdraw their federal registration as an investment adviser?
    a. A newly-formed adviser with $100,000,000 in assets
    b. A long-standing adviser whose AUM has fallen to $98,000,000 after a partner resigns and withdrawals her capital
    c. An adviser whose assets have fallen dramatically as a result of a market correction and capital withdrawals
    d. An adviser whose mutual funds have under performed and its assets are now $85,000,000

10. Which of the following must notify the state securities administrator when an agent changes firms?
    a. The old broker dealer
    b. The agent
    c. The new broker dealer
    d. All of the above

11. Which of the following is true with regard to broker dealers?
    a. A broker dealer may not also be registered as an investment adviser.
    b. A broker dealer may not be an individual.
    c. A broker dealer may also be registered as an investment adviser and may be a corporation or an individual.
    d. A broker dealer may only execute orders for its customers on an agency basis.

12. An investment adviser with $15,000,000 under management and registered with the state must typically keep records readily accessible for:
    a. 2 years.
    b. 3 years.
    c. 5 years.
    d. 10 years.

13. A simplified registration is available for which of the following?
    a. A broker dealer in good standing with a securities regulator in Great Britain
    b. A broker dealer in a neighboring state
    c. A broker dealer in good standing with a Canadian regulator
    d. A broker dealer in good standing with FINRA/NYSE

14. An agent may be denied a registration for all of the following, EXCEPT:
    a. lack of training.
    b. failure to meet financial solvency requirements.
    c. a securities-related misdemeanor.
    d. a court injunction.

15. An investment adviser without custody of funds is subject to all of the following, EXCEPT:
    a. filing fees.
    b. surprise audits.
    c. $35,000 surety bond.
    d. net capital requirements.

16. An investment adviser with no office in the state has given advice to nine individuals in the last 17 months. Which of the following is true?
    a. Because the investment adviser has no office in the state and has given advice to fewer than 10 people, it is not required to register.
    b. An investment adviser is always required to register prior to offering any advice to individuals.
    c. The investment adviser must be registered in this situation even though it has no office in the state.
    d. The investment adviser still qualifies for the de minimis exemption in this case.

CHAPTER 3   Pretest

17. Your client has just opened a wrap account. Which of the following is true?
    a. He will be charged one fee for advice and execution.
    b. He must be given Form ADV Part II.
    c. He must be an accredited investor.
    d. He must deposit at least $150,000 to open the account.

18. All registrations of firms, agents, and advisers:
    a. expire on December 31.
    b. expire after 24 months.
    c. expire after 12 months.
    d. are good for the life of the agent or firm.

CHAPTER 4

Securities Registration, Exempt Securities, and Exempt Transactions

> **INTRODUCTION**
>
> This chapter is typically the section that gives most students a difficult time and may mean the difference between successfully completing the exam and having to retake it at a later time. All securities that are sold to state residents must either be:
>
> - Properly registered;
>   or
> - Exempt from registration;
>   or
> - Sold through an exempt transaction.

EXEMPT SECURITIES

Exempt securities are exempt from the registration requirements of the Securities Act of 1933. Exempt securities are not exempt from the antifraud provisions of the USA. Exempt securities are:

- Issued by exempt issuers, such as governments.
- Short-term debt instruments with less than 270 days to maturity.

SECURITIES REGISTRATION

Nonexempt securities become federally registered by submitting a registration statement to the Securities and Exchange Commission (SEC). Nonexempt securities must also register in the states in which the securities will be sold. The three methods of registering securities in a state are:

1. Coordination
2. Notice filing
3. Qualification

It is important to understand how the three types of securities registration differ and under what circumstances the different registration methods are used.

REGISTRATION OF IPOs THROUGH COORDINATION

When a company first sells stock to the public during an initial public offering (IPO), the company must file a registration statement with the SEC. The company must also file documents with the state securities administrator in the states where the issue will be sold. Most IPOs will register with the state securities administrator at the same time that they register with the SEC. This process of simultaneous registration is known as coordination. The following must be submitted to the administrator:

- Copies of the prospectus
- Any amendments to the prospectus
- The amount of the securities to be offered within the state
- A list of other states where the securities will be offered
- Consent to service of process
- Other information as required by the state securities administrator, including the corporate bylaws, articles of incorporation, specimen of the security, and indenture of any kind

If an amendment has been made to the federal registration, it must also be made to the state registration. A security's state registration will become effective at the time the federal registration becomes effective as long as no stop order has been issued and the documents have been on file with the state for the minimum number of days (usually 10 to 20 days). It is important to note that a state registration may not become effective prior to the security's federal registration becoming effective.

REGISTRATION THROUGH NOTICE FILING

The National Securities Market Improvement Act of 1996 withdrew the states' authority to require the registration of investment companies registered under the Investment Company Act of 1940. The states preserved the right to require investment companies to file a notice and pay a fee. When the issuer of a security notice files with the state securities administrator, the following must be submitted:

- Issuer's name and address
- Type of organization
- Description of the securities to be offered
- Copy of the prospectus
- Copy of documents filed with the SEC
- Consent to service of process
- State fee

Even though the state securities administrator no longer maintains jurisdiction over the registration process of the securities, the administrator still maintains broad investigative powers over any suspected fraudulent sales practices relating to the securities. The administrator may investigate the firms and agents that offer the securities for sale to investors within their state. Notice filing may also be used by other federally covered and federally registered securities that meet the minimum requirements. The administrator may require that an issuer of a federally covered security trading on an exchange file all information with the SEC and submit a consent to service of process prior to offering any securities to state residents. A security that is federally registered and trading on the OTC bulletin board or on the pink sheets may be federally registered but may not meet the minimum criteria to notice file.

REGISTRATION OF NON-ESTABLISHED ISSUERS/ REGISTRATION THROUGH QUALIFICATION

Securities of issuers that do not meet the requirements for registering through notice filing and that are not an IPO must register through qualification. Securities of issuers that will be sold only in one state through an intrastate offering will also be registered through qualification. Registration through qualification is the most complex method of registration. The issuer must file a statement containing all of the information required by the state securities administrator. It may include:

- Name and address of the issuer.
- Type of organization.
- Nature of the issuer's business.
- Description of industry.
- Description of issuer's assets.
- Biographical information on officers and directors, including name, address, compensation, and number of shares owned.
- Type of securities to be offered.
- Price of securities.
- Underwriter's discount.
- Issuer's capitalization and long-term debt.
- Audited balance sheet dated within four months of filing.
- Income statements for three years prior to date of balance sheet.
- Amount and use of proceeds.
- Copy of prospectus or offering circular.
- Copy of advertising and sales literature.
- Specimen of security to be offered.
- Any other information requested by the administrator.
- Consent to service of process.

A securities registration under qualification becomes effective when the administrator so orders.

The following apply to all types of securities registration:

- Registration is effective for up to one year from effective date or until all securities have been sold, whichever is longer.
- State securities administrators set filing fees.
- The registration statement may be amended after its effective date to increase the size of the offering so long as the price and underwriter's compensation remain unchanged.
- The administrator may not require the issuer to file reports more often than quarterly.

- The administrator may require the issuer to report on the progress of the sale of the securities.
- The person who files the registration statement with the state may be the issuer, a broker dealer, or a large stockholder selling shares as part of the offering.

The following apply to registration though coordination and qualification:

- State securities administrators may require that the proceeds from the offering be held in escrow until a certain amount has been sold.
- The administrator may require that the securities be sold on a specific subscription form.

EXEMPT SECURITIES/FEDERALLY COVERED EXEMPTION

The National Securities Market Improvement Act of 1996 provided federally covered exemptions for securities that have met the stringent listing requirements of any U.S. stock exchange, including the Nasdaq stock exchange. An issuer whose common stock is listed on a centralized U.S. stock exchange, such as the NYSE or the Nasdaq stock exchange, is provided an exemption for all of its securities, regardless of their type. An exemption from state registration is also provided to:

- Securities that are sold exclusively to qualified purchasers.
- Investment company securities.
- Securities and transactions exempt from federal registration.
- Debt securities with maturities of less than 270 days and sold in denominations of $50,000 or more.
- Exempt issuers.
- Employee benefit plans.
- Option contracts, both puts and calls on stocks and indexes.
- Equipment trust securities issued by a federally covered or exempt issuer.

Certain securities are exempt from state registration and sales literature requirements because the issuer is exempt. Examples of exempt issuers are:

- U.S. government
- State and municipal governments

- Foreign national governments
- Canadian federal and municipal governments
- Insurance companies
- Banks and trusts
- Credit unions and savings and loans
- Common carriers (railroad, trucking, and airlines) that are subject to the Interstate Commerce Commission (the term "consolidated" is a key word.)
- Religious and charitable organizations
- Public utility securities
- Securities issued by a cooperative

EXEMPT TRANSACTIONS

Sometimes a security that would otherwise have to register is exempt from state registration because of the type of transaction that is involved. The way in which the securities are sold removes the securities from the jurisdiction of the administrator. The following are all exempt transactions.

PRIVATE PLACEMENTS/ REGULATION D OFFERINGS

A private placement is a sale of securities that is made to a group of accredited investors and the securities are not offered to the general public. Accredited investors include institutional investors and individuals who:

- Earn at least $200,000 per year if single;
  or
- Earn at least $300,000 jointly with a spouse;
  or
- Have a net worth of at least $1,000,000 excluding the primary residence.

Sales to nonaccredited investors are limited to 10 in any 12-month period at the state level, and 35 nonaccredited investors at the federal level. No commission may be paid to representatives who sell a private placement to nonaccredited investors (and higher net worth individuals and institutions). All investors in private placements must hold the securities fully paid for at least six months.

The limits on the amount of money that may be raised under the various regulation D offerings are as follows:

Regulation 504 D allows issuers to raise up to $10 million.

Regulation 506 D allows issuers to raise an unlimited amount of capital.

TRANSACTIONS WITH FINANCIAL INSTITUTIONS

All transactions with financial institutions are exempt. The USA was designed to protect the individual investor, not the sophisticated financial institution. Financial institutions include:

- Banks
- Insurance companies
- Investment companies
- Broker dealers
- Pension plans with at least $1,000,000 in assets

TRANSACTIONS WITH FIDUCIARIES

All transactions with fiduciaries are exempt from registration with the administrator. Transactions with any of the following are considered transactions with fiduciaries and are exempt:

- Trustees
- Executors
- Guardians
- Sheriffs/marshals
- Administrators
- Receivers

TRANSACTIONS WITH UNDERWRITERS

All transactions with underwriters of securities are exempt from state registration. For example, if XYZ Corporation is selling 10,000,000 shares of its common stock to its investment bank under a firm commitment underwriting agreement, the transaction is an exempt transaction.

UNSOLICITED ORDERS

All orders that are executed through a broker dealer at the sole request of the customer are considered unsolicited orders, and the securities if not registered within the state are exempt from registration. The administrator may require proof that the order was unsolicited and may require that the customer sign an acknowledgment due to the fact that the unsolicited order is an exempt transaction.

TRANSACTIONS IN MORTGAGE-BACKED SECURITIES

Because of the high quality of the collateral, transactions in mortgage-backed securities are exempt so long as the entire mortgage or deed of trust is sold as a unit in the transaction.

PLEDGES

Should a person pledge securities as collateral for a loan the pledge does not constitute a sale. Additionally, should the borrower default on the loan, the person who now has ownership of the securities by way of default may sell those securities without being required to register the securities to recoup his or her losses.

OFFERS TO EXISTING SECURITIES HOLDERS

Transactions with existing holders of:

- Convertible securities
- Nontransferable warrants
- Transferable warrants exercisable within 90 days

These transactions with existing securities holders are all exempt provided that no commission was paid directly or indirectly for soliciting the security holder.

PREORGANIZATION CERTIFICATES

Certain regulations may require that a corporation receive a minimum level of capital in order to be formed. A preorganization certificate is an agreement to purchase securities prior to the formation of a corporation. The offer or sale of the certificate is exempt if no commission was received for soliciting the sale. The number of subscribers may not exceed 10, and the subscriber may not make any payments.

ISOLATED NONISSUER TRANSACTIONS

An agent or a broker dealer may occasionally recommend a security to a client that is not registered in the client's state of residence as long as it is an isolated event. An isolated transaction means one or very few are performed per year per broker dealer. The number of transactions that qualifies as isolated transactions varies from state to state. An isolated nonissuer transaction may also include a transaction between two individuals without the use of a broker dealer. In this type of transaction, the owner of the securities may sell the securities to another interested party directly.

NONISSUER TRANSACTIONS

A nonissuer transaction is a transaction of publicly traded securities and is exempt if the issuer meets the following requirements:

- The issuer has securities registered under Section 12 of the Securities Exchange Act of 1934 and has been reporting for at least 180 days;

  or

- The issuer has securities registered under the Investment Company Act of 1940;

  or

- The issuer has filed the information required by the Securities Exchange Act of 1934 with the administrator at least 180 days prior to the transaction.

RULE 147 INTRASTATE OFFERING

Rule 147 pertains to offerings of securities that are limited to one state. Because the offering is being made only in one state, it is exempt from registration with the SEC and is subject to the jurisdiction of the state securities administrator.

In order to qualify for an exemption from SEC registration, the issue must be organized and have its principal place of business in the state and meet at least one of the following business criteria:

- 80% of the issuer's income must be received in that state.
- 80% of the offering's proceeds must be used in that state.
- 80% of the issuer's assets must be located in that state.
- A majority of the issuer's employees are based in-state.

All purchasers must be located within the state and must agree not to resell the securities to an out-of-state resident for 6 months.

If the issuer is using an underwriter, the broker dealer must have an office in that state.

The SEC has also adopted Rule 147A, which is largely identical to Rule 147. However, Rule 147A allows companies that are incorporated or organized out of state to use the Rule 147 exemption. Rule 147 A also allows issuers to use the internet and to advertise securities being offered through rule 147. Additionally, offers may be made to purchasers while they are out of state. However, all sales are still limited to investors residing in the state where the offering is being conducted.

CHAPTER 4

Pretest

SECURITIES REGISTRATION, EXEMPT SECURITIES, AND EXEMPT TRANSACTIONS

1. A broker dealer sells a nonexempt unregistered security to an investment company. Which of the following is true?
   a. This is a prohibited practice.
   b. The broker dealer must offer rescission.
   c. This is an exempt transaction.
   d. This is a nonexempt transaction.

2. A registered representative may sell a nonexempt unregistered security in which of the following instances?
   a. An IPO
   b. A private placement
   c. In a wash sale
   d. During arbitrage transactions only

3. Which of the following is an exempt transaction?
   a. A transaction involving $100,000 worth of Treasury bonds
   b. A transaction involving commercial paper
   c. A transaction involving an unsolicited order
   d. A transaction involving a common stock listed on the NYSE

4. Commercial paper must be issued in which of the following to be considered an exempt security?
   I. Denominations of less than $50,000
   II. Denominations of more than $50,000
   III. A maturity of less than 270 days
   IV. Be issued by a bank
   a. I, III, and IV
   b. II and III
   c. II, III, and IV
   d. II and III

5. A large broker dealer has recommended a nonexempt unregistered security to three individual investors in the last 12 months. According to the USA this is:
   a. a violation, and the broker dealer must offer rescission to the customers involved.
   b. a violation of both state and federal laws, and the broker dealer may be fined, sanctioned, or both.
   c. examples of isolated nonissuer transactions, and the transactions are exempt.
   d. examples of unsolicited orders for government or municipal securities, and the securities are exempt from registration.

6. Which of the following is NOT a federally covered security?
   a. A stock listed on the NYSE
   b. Shares of an investment company
   c. Common stock that has been duly registered within the state through filing
   d. A common stock listed on the Nasdaq Capital Market

7. Under the USA, transactions with which of the following are NOT exempt?
   a. Weathly investors
   b. Trustees
   c. Administrators
   d. Underwriters

CHAPTER 4 Pretest

8. All of the following are exempt from state registration, EXCEPT:
   a. common stock of Houston Power and Light Co.
   b. common stock of XYZ Consolidated.
   c. warrants of ALG Company. ALG's common stock is listed on the American Stock Exchange.
   d. XYZ common stock listed on the Vancouver Stock Exchange.

9. A securities state registration becomes effective under coordination after a maximum of:
   a. 10 days.
   b. 30 days.
   c. 25 days.
   d. 20 days.

10. A broker dealer distributing a private placement may sell the offering to how many nonaccredited investors?
    a. No more than 35 in 12 months
    b. No more than 10 in 12 months
    c. No more than 15 in 12 months
    d. No more than 10 in 6 months

11. Which of the following becomes effective at the same time as the SEC registration?
    a. Qualification
    b. Coordination
    c. Application
    d. Notification

12. Which of the following is NOT an exempt transaction?
    a. A transaction involving $4,200 worth of securities executed at the customer's request
    b. Sales of unregistered securities to an investment company
    c. Recommendation to an individual investor to purchase 500 shares of XYZ. XYZ is listed on the NYSE
    d. An issuer sells 5,000,000 shares of common stock to its underwriter

13. All of the following are ways to register a security within a state, EXCEPT for:
    a. application.
    b. notification.
    c. qualification.
    d. coordination.

14. Which of the following is t.rue of a federally covered security?
    a. It is exempt from both SEC and state registration.
    b. It is only issued by exempt issuers.
    c. It is not required to register with the state securities administrator.
    d. It has a maximum maturity of 270 days.

15. All of the following issuers are exempt from state registration, EXCEPT for:
    a. the London Bridge and Tunnel Authority.
    b. New Mexico.
    c. Ontario.
    d. the Russian government.

16. An issuer whose registration has already become effective with the SEC will most likely register its securities with the state securities administrator through:
    a. coordination.
    b. application.
    c. notification.
    d. qualification.

CHAPTER 4 Pretest

17. The term "isolated nonissuer transaction" relates to transactions between state residents executed through wh.ich of the following?
    - I. An underwriter
    - II. A broker dealer
    - III. A government
    - IV. An investment adviser

    a. I and III
    b. II and IV
    c. III and IV
    d. I, II, III, and IV

18. Which of the following is an exempt transaction?
    a. Transactions with high net worth clients within the state
    b. Sale of 30-year Treasury bonds to the account of a conservative investor
    c. Transaction with a trust administrator
    d. The sale of a convertible bond to a long-term investor

CHAPTER 5

Professional Conduct and Prohibited and Fraudulent Actions

> ### INTRODUCTION
>
> The largest portion of the Series 63 exam comprises questions that require you to identify fraudulent and prohibited practices. Some are easy to identify just by applying proper business ethics. Other questions require more thought to determine if a violation has occurred. The Series 63 exam is based on the laws of the Uniform Securities Act (USA), and all candidates must be able to apply the laws correctly in a variety of situations.

FRAUD

Fraud is defined as any act that is employed to obtain an unfair advantage over another party. Fraud includes:

- False statements.
- Deliberate omissions of material facts.
- Concealment of material facts.
- Manipulative and deceptive practices.

PROFESSIONAL CONDUCT

All industry participants are expected to uphold high professional standards and to adhere to just and equitable practices. All broker dealers, investment advisers, and agents are prohibited from:

- Implying that any securities regulator has approved or endorsed any security, firm, or agent.
- Misrepresenting an account status or commissions to be charged.
- Making inaccurate market quotes.
- Misrepresenting a company's earnings.
- Guaranteeing results or promising "no loss."
- Making predictions about a security's future performance without clearly stating that it is an opinion and not a fact.
- Stating that a security will be listed on an exchange without knowledge of such listing.
- Trading or making recommendations based on inside information.
- Manipulating the market for a security.
- Unreasonably delaying a customer's request that a check or certificate be sent to them.
- Splitting or sharing commissions or advisory fees with individuals who are not properly registered.
- Offering free services without the intent to provide or charging a fee for the free service.

SUITABILITY

A representative must ensure that all recommendations are suitable for the customer based on an investigation of the customer's investment objectives, financial profile, and attitude toward investing. A recommendation to a customer could be profitable yet still be unsuitable if the customer's profile is considered. Firms and agents are prohibited from:

- Making blanket recommendations.
- Churning customer's accounts.

- Making unfair comparisons.
- Making recommendations that do not meet the client's investment objective or investment profile.
- Selling away.
- Making recommendations that are excessive in size based on the customer's ability to pay.

EXAMPLE

Mr. Jones, an agent with XYZ Brokers, has a large customer base that ranges from young investors who are just starting to save to institutions and retirees. Mr. Jones has been doing a significant amount of research on WSIA industries, a mining and materials company. Mr. Jones strongly believes that WSIA is significantly undervalued based on its assets and earning potential. Mr. Jones recommends WSIA to all his clients. In the next six months the share price of WSIA increases significantly as new production dramatically increases sales, just as Mr. Jones' research suggested. The clients then sell WSIA at Mr. Jones' suggestion and realize a significant profit.

ANALYSIS

Even though the clients who purchased WSIA based on Mr. Jones's recommendation made a significant profit, Mr. Jones has still committed a violation because he recommended it to all of his clients. Mr. Jones's clients have a wide variety of investment objectives, and the risk or income potential associated with an investment in WSIA would not be suitable for every client. Even if an investment is profitable for the client it does not mean it was suitable for the client. Blanket recommendations are never suitable.

TAKENOTE!

An investment adviser who has discretion over client accounts may in certain circumstances be found to have made unsuitable blanket recommendations if the adviser purchases a significant amount of an illiquid security for a large number of client accounts. This action could also be deemed to be market manipulation.

MARKET MANIPULATION

It is unlawful for a firm or an agent to engage in any activity that is designed to control or influence a security's price or activity. Manipulative practices include:

- Capping.
- Pegging.
- Front running.
- Trading ahead.
- Wash sales/matched purchases/matched sales/painting the tape.
- Participating in rings or pools.

Capping: A manipulative act designed to keep a stock price from rising or to keep the price down.

Pegging: A manipulative act designed to keep a stock price up or to keep the price from falling.

Front running: The entering of an order for the account of an agent or firm prior to the entering of a large customer order. The firm or agent is using the customer's order to profit on the order it has entered for its own account.

Trading ahead: The entering of an order for a security based on the prior knowledge of a soon to be released research report.

Painting the tape: A manipulative act by two or more parties designed to create false activity in the security without any beneficial change in ownership. The increased activity is used to attract new buyers.

Participating in rings or pools: Investors many not act in concert to manipulate the price of a security or for the purpose of concealing the actual ownership or control of the security.

Firms and agents are also prohibited from:

- Commingling customers' cash and securities with the firm's or agent's securities.
- Borrowing money or securities from a customer unless the customer is a bank or other lending institution.
- Accepting orders from a third party not named on the account.
- Affecting unauthorized transactions.

- Engaging in nondisclosed private securities transactions without the firm's permission.
- Using discretionary authority without obtaining discretionary authority in writing.
- Not disclosing a customer's written complaints to a principal of the firm.
- Not disclosing a larger than ordinary commission.
- Sharing in the profit or loss of a customer's account with no investment in the account.
- Spreading rumors.
- Using flamboyant language.
- Promising services with no intent or ability to perform.
- Recommending unregistered nonexempt securities.
- Backdating records.

CUSTOMER COMPLAINTS

All written complaints received from a customer or from an individual acting on behalf of the customer must be reported promptly to the principal of the firm. The firm must maintain a separate customer complaint folder, even if it has not received any written customer complaints. If the firm's file contains complaints, the file must state what action was taken by the firm, if any, and it must disclose the location of the file containing any correspondence relating to the complaint. When a written complaint is received by mail or email, the customer who has issued the complaint must be notified that the complaint has been received. If a customer files a complaint and subsequently withdraws the complaint, the firm is still requested to maintain the correspondence relating to the complaint in the firm's complaint file.

THE ROLE OF THE INVESTMENT ADVISER

An investment adviser charges a fee for his or her services for advising clients as to the value of securities or for making recommendations as to which securities should be purchased or sold. Unlike a broker dealer, the investment adviser has a contractual relationship with his or her clients and must always adhere to the highest standards of professional conduct.

ADDITIONAL COMPENSATION FOR AN INVESTMENT ADVISER

In addition to the fees charged by an investment adviser, an investment adviser may also:

- Receive commissions for executing a customer's transaction through certain broker dealers.
- Act as a principal in a customer's transaction.

The above sources of additional revenue must be disclosed to the client in writing prior to the investment adviser completing such transactions. For this rule, completion of the transaction occurs on the settlement date.

AGENCY CROSS TRANSACTIONS

An agency cross transaction is one in which the investment adviser represents both the purchasing and selling security holder either as an investment adviser or as a broker dealer. If the investment adviser is going to execute an agency cross transaction, the adviser must get the advisory client's authorization in writing. The authorization may be pulled at any time verbally, and the adviser may not have solicited both sides of the trade. The investment adviser still maintains a duty to obtain the best execution for both clients and may not execute the cross at a price that favors one client over the other. The adviser must send notice to its clients annually detailing the number of all agency cross transactions completed by the adviser.

DISCLOSURES BY AN INVESTMENT ADVISER

An investment adviser must update its form ADV annually within 90 days of its fiscal year end. Additionally, the investment adviser must provide each client with an updated brochure annually within 120 days of the adviser's fiscal year end. The brochure must be provided free of charge and must provide a summary of material changes to the advisory firm.

An investment adviser must disclose all of the following:

- Conflicts of interest
- Sources of recommendations

- Location of customer's funds for advisers with custody
- Any legal actions taken against the adviser
- Material facts
- Soft dollar arrangements

If the change to the investment adviser's business is material, it must be disclosed promptly. It is critical that you know what changes to the investment advisory firm are deemed material and when those changes must be disclosed. Most investment advisory firms other than small sole proprietorships are organized either as corporations or as partnerships. A material change to the ownership or control of the adviser is considered to be material and must be disclosed promptly. If the adviser is a corporation and one of the firm's major stockholders sells, pledges, or assigns its block of controlling voting shares, then this would be seen as both material and as an assignment of the contract, and it must be disclosed promptly. If the nature of the transfer is deemed to be an assignment, the client would have to give consent to continue the relationship. However, if an officer of the corporation leaves, then no disclosure is required. If the advisory firm is organized as a partnership and a major partner dies or departs from the partnership, this would be considered material and as an assignment. Therefore, the material change must be disclosed promptly, and the client must give consent to continue the advisory relationship. However, if the partnership adds or removes minority partners, then these events would not be deemed material.

An investment adviser may not:

- Borrow from a customer.
- Commingle customer's funds with the adviser's funds.
- Accept an order from a party not named on the account of the customer.
- Churn customer accounts.
- Make unsuitable recommendations.
- Charge unreasonable fees.

An investment adviser with custody of customers' funds must:

- Segregate all customer funds and securities.
- Give the customer a written notice of the location of the funds.
- Establish a separate bank account for the customers' funds.

- Provide quarterly statements showing all transactions and account status.
- Go through an annual surprise audit.

INVESTMENT ADVISER CONTRACTS

All investment adviser contracts must be in writing and must contain disclosures of:

- Length of the contract.
- Services to be provided.
- Fees to be charged and how they are assessed.
- The amount of any prepaid fees to be returned upon cancellation of the contract.
- A statement prohibiting the investment adviser from assigning the contract without the customer's consent.
- A notification of any changes in the adviser's management.
- Limits on the adviser's discretionary authority over the customer's account, if any.

SEC MARKETING RULES FOR INVESTMENT ADVISERS

The SEC has modernized the advertising rules for investment advisers. The new rule sets standards regarding the use of testimonials, performance-based presentations and the use of third-party rating systems. The term advertisement as defined under The Advisers Marketing Rule includes any direct or indirect communications made by the adviser that offers advisory services with regard to securities to prospective clients or to prospective private fund investors. Also included in the definition of an advertisement, is the offering of additional services to current clients or to current private fund investors. Most one-on-one communications between the adviser and clients or prospective clients are specifically excluded from the definition of an advertisement. Testimonials and endorsements are classified as advertising and are prohibited unless the adviser makes certain required disclosures. These required disclosures include:

- The advertisement must clearly and prominently disclose if the person or promoter, is a client or has received any compensation for providing his / her testimonial or endorsement.

- The adviser who uses testimonials or endorsements in advertising must ensure compliance with the adviser marketing rule

- The adviser is required to enter into a written contract or agreement with the person providing his or her testimonial or endorsement unless the promoter is an affiliate of the adviser or when compensation does not exceed $1,000 during the preceding 12 months.

It's important to note that the compensation received by a promoter may be received in the form of cash or in other forms of non cash compensation. Reduced advisory fees, directed brokerage transactions, awards or prizes are all considered to be compensation. If the value of the non-cash compensation exceeds $1,000, the adviser must enter into a written agreement with the promoter unless the promoter is an affiliate of the adviser.

The use of third-party rating systems and citing adviser performance is strictly regulated under the adviser marketing rule. Advisers who provide this information are required to adhere to the following guidelines:

- Advisers are prohibited from including third-party ratings in an advertisement unless the adviser provides disclosures and has satisfied certain criteria regarding the preparation of the rating

- Advisers may not cite gross performance data unless the adviser also provides net performance data in its advertisements

- Advisers may not cite past performance data unless the performance is provided for a specific time.

- Advisers who cite performance data must provide the performance data for all portfolios with similar investment policies, objectives and strategies as those being offered in the advertisement

- Unless generated by an interactive analysis tool, advisers are prohibited from providing hypothetical performance data unless the adviser implements policies and procedures designed to ensure that the hypothetical performance data is relevant to the financial situation and investment objectives of the intended audience and provides relevant data regarding the hypothetical performance

- An adviser who has acquired another advisory firm may not cite the performance of the predecessor unless the accounts and personnel of the advertising adviser are similar to the accounts and personnel of the predecessor adviser

In addition to the above rules and regulations the marketing rule provides general prohibitions with regard to an adviser's conduct, including:
- Making any untrue, false or misleading statements

- Omitting a material fact

- Making any statement or including information that would cause an untrue or misleading implication or inference to be drawn concerning a material fact relating to the adviser

- Making statements regarding potential returns or rewards without balancing the statements with a discussion of the potential risks and limitations of the investments

- Including or excluding performance results or presenting performance for time periods that would make the illustration unfair or unbalanced

- Including any information that would make statements false or materially misleading

- Making any representation that the SEC or any regulator endorses or approves the adviser

PRIVATE INVESTMENT COMPANIES/HEDGE FUNDS

A private investment company may charge performance-based compensation to clients provided that the clients have a minimum of $1,000,000 of assets under the adviser's management or have a net worth of $2,000,000.

FULCRUM FEES

Advisers who manage accounts for investment companies or accounts with a value greater than $1 million, if those accounts are not for trusts or retirement plans, may charge fulcrum fees. A fulcrum fee provides the adviser with additional compensation for outperforming a broad-based index such as the S&P 500 and less compensation for underperforming the index. The amount of the additional compensation received for outperforming the index must be equal to the amount of compensation that would be lost for underperformance. The index used as the basis to determine the adviser's performance must contain similar securities and risks.

SOFT DOLLARS

Brokerage firms will often provide investment advisers with services that go beyond execution and research. These services are provided in exchange for commission business and are known as soft dollars. The services received should normally be research related. However, in some instances the services received are used for other purposes and benefit the adviser. In order for the soft dollar arrangement to include the safe harbor provisions, investment advisers must ensure that the services received are for the benefit of the client and pay careful attention to the disclosure requirements relating to all soft dollar arraignments. If an adviser receives soft dollar compensation from a broker dealer to whom the adviser directs customer transactions (known as directed transactions) the adviser must disclose any arrangement to clients. The fees charged to execute the transactions should by fair and reasonable, in line with what is available in the marketplace and in line with the value of the services offered to the adviser and its clients. The execution fees are not required to be the lowest, and simply using a broker dealer whose services are more expensive will not constitute a breach of the adviser's fiduciary duty. If the adviser directs transactions to a broker dealer in exchange for services that benefit the adviser, the adviser must disclose all facts relating to the arrangement and receive the client's written consent to enter into the arrangement even if such arrangement does not increase the costs to the client. If the adviser selects broker dealers to execute client orders based on the research or other services provided, it must be disclosed on form ADV.

The SEC has divided soft dollar considerations into the following categories:

- Goods/services
- Accounting fees
- Association membership fees
- Cable and television
- Commission rebates
- Computer hardware
- Computer software
- Conferences/seminars
- Consulting services
- Courier/postage/express mail
- Custodial fees
- Electronic databases
- Employee salary/benefits
- Execution assistance
- Industry publications
- Legal fees
- Management fees
- Miscellaneous expenses
- Office equipment/supplies
- Online quotation and news services
- Portfolio management software
- Rent
- Research/analysis reports
- Telephone expenses
- Travel expenses
- Tuition/training costs
- Utilities expenses

 TAKENOTE!

Only the items that can truly be deemed to be for the benefit of the client are within the safe harbor. Valuation software and other research related items are within the safe harbor, while paying for a laptop or rent for the adviser would not be within the safe harbor.

BORROWING AND LENDING MONEY

The borrowing and lending of money between registered persons and customers is strictly regulated. If the broker dealer allows borrowing and lending between representatives and customers, the firm must have policies in place that will allow for the loans to be made. Loans may be made between an agent or a customer if the customer is a bank or other lending institution, where there is a personal or outside business relationship and that relationship is the basis for the loan, or between two agents registered with the same firm. If an agent wishes to maintain a joint account with an adult customer, the firm may allow an agent to do so as long as the agent's participation in the profits and losses of the account are in direct relation to their financial contribution to the account.

FREE SERVICES

If a member firm advertises free services to customers or to people who respond to an ad, the services must actually be free to everyone and with no strings attached.

FREE LUNCH SEMINARS

The practice of providing so-called free lunch seminars presents several unique compliance concerns. Firms that sponsor seminars that are marketed to investors as educational workshops often provide attendees with a "free lunch" as a way to help market the seminar and state that "no investment products will be offered or sold" at the seminar. However, firms who sponsor these seminars clearly intend to establish a business relationship with the attendees. The firms may try to get the attendees to open an account either at the seminar or during a follow-up solicitation to offer investment products. Firms who sponsor free lunch seminars must ensure that strict compliance procedures are followed by the agents who lead the seminars. Without strict compliance to conduct and disclosures rules, The North American Securities Administrators Association/NASAA considers free lunch seminars a prohibited practice. Of particular concern are seminars that are marketed to seniors.

CHAPTER 5

Pretest

PROFESSIONAL CONDUCT AND PROHIBITED AND FRAUDULENT ACTIONS

1. All of the following are always a violation, EXCEPT:
   a. inaccurate market quotes.
   b. implying that a regulator has approved a security.
   c. charging a larger than ordinary commission.
   d. not stating material facts.

2. With regard to a representative's management of an account, which of the following is strictly prohibited?
   a. A third party executing an order for a client with proper trading authorization
   b. A spouse of a client instructing a representative to invest $5,000 into a balanced mutual fund
   c. A representative borrowing money from a client, New York Superior Bank
   d. A client having a joint account with a representative

3. Two or more people who engage in a pattern of buying and selling a security between themselves to attract new investors are engaging in a fraudulent act known as:
   a. arbitrage.
   b. painting the tape.
   c. churning.
   d. trading ahead.

4. During an advertisement, a firm makes an offer of free services to anyone who responds to the ad. A prospective client responding to the ad is informed that there is a $49.95 handling fee. This is:
   a. acceptable, as long as it is applied to all people who respond to the ad.
   b. a violation, because an advertisement of free services must be totally free with no strings attached.
   c. a violation, because the fee is excessive.
   d. permitted only to cover shipping and handling.

5. A broker who has been on the phone with a customer who is complaining about the representative's service must:
   a. notify the principal of the firm.
   b. offer additional services free of charge to the customer.
   c. offer to lower his fees.
   d. do nothing.

6. An agent writes a check to pay for a purchase of securities in an account that she shares with a friend. Which of the following is true?
   a. This is commingling and is not allowed under any circumstances.
   b. This is permitted for joint accounts approved by a principal of the firm.
   c. This is only permitted if the other party is the agent's spouse.
   d. The representative is lending money to the other party, which is a violation.

7. Which of the following is a violation?
   a. An agent recommends a balanced mutual fund with good historical performance to all of his clients.
   b. A client is charged a larger than ordinary commission to accumulate a position in municipal bonds.
   c. A broker dealer charges a nonactive account fee of $75 only to accounts that have executed fewer than three trades in the last 12 months.
   d. A broker dealer sells an unregistered nonexempt security to several clients over a 14-month period.

8. An agent offers to constantly monitor a client's account during market hours. This is:
   a. required of agents.
   b. an example of a "full service" brokerage firm.
   c. a violation.
   d. justification for higher commissions.

9. An agent is actively soliciting orders for unregistered exempt securities. Which of the following is true?
   a. This is a flagrant violation of the USA, and the agent may be held both civilly and criminally liable.
   b. This is an acceptable practice.
   c. The administrator may issue a cease and desist order.
   d. The agent's registration may be suspended or revoked by the administrator.

10. An agent advises a client to purchase an interest in a privately offered limited partnership not sponsored by her firm and without the firm's knowledge. The agent has:
    a. acted appropriately by finding a suitable investment for her client.
    b. defrauded her firm of its commission for the transaction.
    c. committed a felony.
    d. committed a violation known as selling away.

11. A client makes the maximum contribution to his IRA and at the same time makes the maximum contribution to his nonworking spouse's IRA. The client then instructs the representative to invest the contributions in both accounts in a growth mutual fund. The representative should:
    a. accept the order and invest the money as requested.
    b. accept only the order for the client's account.
    c. accept both orders and confirm the order with the spouse at a later time.
    d. instruct the client that he would be better off opening a joint IRA.

12. While visiting the offices of a company that he has been recommending to a large number of clients, a representative overhears that the company will have to restate its earnings for the last two years and report a loss for those periods instead of a profit. Which of the following may the representative do?

    I. Call all of his clients and advise them to sell but not state the reason for the recommendation.
    II. Discuss the situation with his principal.
    III. Stop recommending the security.
    IV. Accept an unsolicited order to buy or sell the security.

    a. I and II
    b. II and III
    c. III and IV
    d. II, III, and IV

13. An agent tells a client that an exempt security is not required to register because it is safer than a nonexempt security. Which of the following is true?

    I. The agent has accurately advised their client as to the safety of the investment.
    II. The agent has misrepresented the investment risks of the security.
    III. The agent has committed a violation.
    IV. The agent could be liable for misrepresentation of the security.

    a. I only
    b. II and IV
    c. III and IV
    d. II, III, and IV

14. With regard to discretionary accounts, which of the following is NOT true?

    a. Discretionary authorization must be in writing.
    b. All purchases must be in line with the client's objectives.
    c. The customer may reject any purchase after reviewing it.
    d. The representative may be held liable for unsuitable recommendations.

15. Which of the following is NOT an example of market manipulation?
    a. Participating in rings or pools
    b. A market maker selling a security to a customer at the offer after just purchasing it at the bid for his own account
    c. Engaging in transactions that result in no beneficial change in ownership
    d. Purchasing a security at the offer at the close of the market to increase its price

16. An agent at a brokerage firm recommends a stock to a client. The brokerage firm is owned by the company whose shares the agent is recommending. The company is considered a "blue-chip" company. Which of the following is true?
    a. The agent must disclose the control relationship in writing.
    b. Because the company is considered a "blue-chip" company, no additional disclosure is required.
    c. The agent must disclose the control relationship prior to the purchase of the securities.
    d. The USA does not concern itself with control relationships of issuers who qualify for the "blue-chip" exemption.

17. An agent has worked closely with an issuer and feels that the company will report better than expected earnings tomorrow. A client calls and tells the representative to sell the stock at the market. The agent, feeling that the report will cause the stock to rise dramatically, waits to sell the stock until after the earnings report. The next day the stock rises dramatically, and the agent sells the stock for the client at a much higher price. This is an example of which of the following?
    a. An informed representative servicing a client's account
    b. A violation for failing to follow a customer's instructions
    c. A full-service firm servicing its customer's account
    d. Market timing on the part of the representative

18. An agent recommends a security to a large financial firm. In doing so, the representative omits a material fact in order to make a brief presentation because the customer is an institutional investor. Which of the following is true?
    a. The representative may make a brief presentation that omits material facts because the USA does not concern itself with institutional investors.
    b. The representative has committed a violation by omitting material facts.
    c. Institutional investors do their own research and may accept limited recommendations made by representatives.
    d. Institutional investors usually make investment decisions based on market momentum, so the representative's recommendation was appropriate.

19. Which of the following statements made by a representative is a violation?
    I. A representative tells a customer that the principal on the Treasury bonds in his account is guaranteed by the U.S. government.
    II. A representative tells a customer to purchase XYZ because the price will go up over the long term.
    III. A representative tells a customer that the corporate bonds that she has purchased have been guaranteed by the company's parent company.
    IV. A representative informs a customer that the "talk on the street" is that the company is going to come out with a revolutionary new product.
    a. I and II
    b. II and III
    c. II and IV
    d. II, III, and IV

20. An agent without discretionary authority over a client's account may accept which of the following orders?
    a. A client asks the agent to purchase 500 shares of XYZ whenever he thinks the price is right.
    b. A client's spouse calls and tells the agent that the client has been called out of town for a family emergency and needs to liquidate $5,000 worth of securities to meet the unexpected expense.
    c. A client asks the agent to purchase 500 shares of whatever stock he feels offers the most growth potential over the next 12 months.
    d. The client's attorney calls and asks the agent to liquidate $10,000 worth of securities to cover part of the down payment on the client's new home.

CHAPTER 6

The State Securities Administrator and the Uniform Securities Act

INTRODUCTION

The state securities administrator has the authority to enforce all of the provisions of the Uniform Securities Act (USA) within the administrator's state. The state securities administrator may deny, revoke, or suspend the registration of a security, an agent, or a firm. The administrator may also revoke an exemption from registration, subpoena and investigate any registrant, and amend rules as required. The administrator's rules and orders have the same authority as any part of the USA, but the administrator's rules and orders do not become part of the USA. The USA requires the administrator to publish all rules and orders.

ACTIONS BY THE STATE SECURITIES ADMINISTRATOR

A state securities administrator may take action to bar, suspend, censure, or restrict the activities of a registrant if the administrator finds it to be in the public interest and the applicant or registrant does one or more of the following:

- Fails to pay filing fees
- Is insolvent

- Fails to supervise employees
- Willfully violates the securities or banking laws of another country or has had a foreign regulator deny, revoke, or suspend its registration within the last five years
- Violates federal securities or commodities laws
- Has been convicted of any felony within the last 10 years
- Has been convicted of a securities-related misdemeanor
- Willfully violates any provision of the USA
- Files an incomplete, false, or misleading application for registration
- Has been temporarily or permanently enjoined from the securities business by a court of law
- Has been subject to an order by a state securities administrator denying, revoking, or suspending its registration
- Is deemed unqualified due to a lack of experience, training, or knowledge
- Engages in unethical or dishonest business practices

The administrator deeming it is in the public interest is not enough to take action. The applicant must have been involved in one or more of the activities listed above. If the administrator is going to take action against the applicant, the applicant must be promptly notified in writing of the administrator's intention. The administrator must also provide a hearing for the applicant within 15 days of receiving the request for a hearing. Although an administrator may deny an applicant's registration based on the applicant's lack of knowledge, training, or experience, a lack of experience may not be the sole basis for the denial of a registration.

CANCELLATION OF A REGISTRATION

The administrator may cancel the registration of a broker dealer, investment adviser, or an agent if the registrant or applicant no longer exists, has ceased doing business, or cannot be located. If, for example, the administrator sends a notice to a registrant and the notice is returned to the administrator as undeliverable with no known forwarding address, the administrator would have reasonable grounds for canceling the registrations. Additionally, an individual's registration may be canceled if the person has been deemed mentally incompetent by a court of law. The cancellation of a registration by the administrator is not a disciplinary or punitive action; it is more clerical in nature.

WITHDRAWAL OF A REGISTRATION

A broker dealer, investment adviser, or an agent may request that his or her registration with the state be withdrawn. The withdrawal will become effective 30 days after the administrator receives the request if no revocation or suspension proceedings are in process. The administrator has up to one year after the withdrawal of an applicant's registration to take action against the applicant to suspend or revoke the registration.

ACTIONS AGAINST AN ISSUER OF SECURITIES

The administrator may deny, revoke, or suspend the registration of a security if it deems it is in the public interest and:

- Any officer or director has been convicted of a securities crime.
- The registration statement is false, misleading, or incomplete.
- The security is subject to a court injunction.
- The promoter's fees or offering expenses are excessive or unreasonable.
- The offering is fraudulent.

The administrator may also revoke a security's exemption from registration if it is in the public interest and the exemption was based on a false, misleading, fraudulent, or unethical practice or statement. An administrator may, without prior notice, revoke the exempt status of a securities transaction.

RULE CHANGES

An administrator may change or amend rules as he or she deems necessary. All rules enacted by the administrator will have the same force and effect as rules enacted under the USA. An administrator's order may be appealed to the court system within 60 days by any aggrieved party. The appeal will not act as a temporary stay to the administrator's order unless first so ordered by a court. A rule enacted by the administrator applies to all registrants in the administrator's state.

ADMINISTRATIVE ORDERS

If the state securities administrator issues an order, that order will be enforced against a specific registrant or activity. For example, if a broker dealer was engaging in sales practices that violated the USA, the administrator could issue an order suspending that broker dealer's registration with the state for 60 days. Any affected party may challenge an administrator's order within 60 days of issuance by filing a written petition. During the time that the challenge is pending the order will remain in effect. If the administrator determines that the order is no longer required or a court determines that the order is no longer required, the administrator's order will be vacated.

An administrator may enter an order against a registered firm agent or security without holding a hearing. This is known as a summary order. A summary order may be issues in any of the following circumstances:

- To deny or revoke the exemption from registration of a security or transaction
- To postpone or suspend the registration of an agent during an investigation of a potential violation or registration issue pending a final decision
- To postpone or suspend the registration of a security during an investigation of a potential violation or registration issue pending a final decision

If the administrator enters an order on a summary basis the administrator must send notice to all parties against whom the order was entered. The notice must provide the details of the order as well as the reasons for entering the order. The parties must also be notified that a hearing will be granted within 15 days of receipt of a written request. Once an order becomes final, the administrator must provide a detail of all facts that lead to the order and the legal basis for the order. No order entered by the administrator may become final without prior written notice and the opportunity for a hearing. The administrator's order may be appealed to the court system within 60 days. The appeal will not act as a stay of the order unless a court issues a stay.

 TAKENOTE!

If the administrator suspends the registration of a firm all of the individuals who are registered with the firm will have their registrations placed in suspense status. After the term of suspension has been completed all registrations will be reactivated. If the firm's registration had been revoked all individuals whose registrations were not revoked would be required to find a new firm to become associated with.

CHAPTER 6 The State Securities Administrator and the Uniform Securities Act

A stop order is an administrative order taken against an issuer of security that stops the security from being sold in the administrator's state. If the issuer cures or corrects the deficiency or problem with the security the stop order will be lifted and the security will be allowed to be sold. A cease and desist order is an order against a person or firm who is engaging in or about to engage in an activity the administrator deems unacceptable.

INTERPRETIVE OPINIONS

A person who is actively engaged in the securities business may from time to time seek the opinion of the state securities administrator to ensure that the business being conducted is in line with the rules of the USA as amended within the state. In response to the request, the administrator may issue an opinion regarding the activity, issue a no-action letter, or elect not to issue an opinion. If the administrator issues an interpretive opinion, the administrator may charge a fee for the interpretation of the state's rules.

ADMINISTRATIVE RECORDS

The state securities administrator will maintain all records relating to the business of the state securities administrator and will make the records available upon request. The administrator will provide certified copies if specifically requested. The administrator may charge a reasonable fee for the production and delivery of the records. The records to be maintained include:

- All applications for broker dealer registration.
- All applications for investment adviser registration.
- All applications for agent registration for broker dealers and investment advisers.
- All applications for registrations of securities and registration statements.
- All orders, actions, and interpretive opinions entered.
- All written claims for exemptions from registration.

The records may be maintained electronically, on microfilm, or on any other device the administrator may elect.

INVESTIGATIONS

A state securities administrator may investigate a broker dealer, a state investment adviser, or an agent in any state if the administrator believes that a violation has taken or may take place. The administrator may also subpoena people, books, and records in any state and may administer oaths to compel people to testify. Anyone who displays contempt for the administrator's order is guilty of contumacy and may be found in contempt of court if the administrator asks the court to enforce its orders.

> **TAKENOTE!**
>
> While the administrator may investigate and take action in all of the above situations, the administrator does not have jurisdiction over activities that take place exclusively outside of the administrator's state.

CIVIL AND CRIMINAL PENALTIES

A state securities administrator may issue a cease and desist order without a prior hearing or notice. The administrator may appoint a receiver to oversee the assets of violators and may require them to make restitution. The administrator does not have the power to arrest anyone and must refer the case to the attorney general or other office empowered to make arrests. Anyone who is found to have knowingly and willfully criminally violated the laws of the USA is subject to a $5,000 fine and/or three years in prison. People who criminally violate the Investment Advisers Act of 1940 are subject to a $10,000 fine and/or five years in prison. The statute of limitations for an administrator taking action is five years.

An investor who sues for a violation of the Uniform Securities Act is entitled to receive:

- The value that they paid for the securities minus any income received during the holding period (e.g., dividends).
- Interest on their money for the holding period.
- Court costs.

Civil actions may be taken against:

- An agent.
- A firm.
- The agent's supervisor.

If an investment adviser violates the provisions of the USA, clients may sue to recover:

- Advisory fees.
- Losses.
- Interest on the money.
- Attorney fees and court costs, minus any income received as a result of the advice.

JURISDICTION OF THE STATE SECURITIES ADMINISTRATOR

Whereas the USA sets forth model legislation for state securities laws, it is the responsibility of the state securities administrator to administer the laws within a particular state.

The powers granted to the administrator under the Uniform Securities Act include the ability to:

- Cancel, deny, suspend, or revoke a registration of an agent, firm, or security.
- Cancel, deny, suspend, or revoke an exemption from registration of an agent, firm, or security.
- Conduct investigations.
- Issue subpoenas.
- Issue cease and desist orders.
- Seek injunctions.
- Amend, make, and rescind rules and orders.

The only time that a state securities administrator has any authority to investigate a federally registered investment adviser is if the adviser's principal office is located within the administrator's state. The principal office is where the executive and C-level directors maintain offices.

ADMINISTRATOR'S JURISDICTION OVER SECURITIES TRANSACTIONS

The state securities administrator has jurisdiction over securities transactions that:

- Originated within the state.
- Are directed into the state.
- Are accepted in the state.

If a client draws a check on an out-of-state bank or has the securities sent to another state, this does not give the securities administrator in those states jurisdiction.

The offer and acceptance of a security constitutes a transaction or the sale of a security. It is the actual conveyance of the ownership of the security for value.

> **TESTFOCUS!**
>
> Mr. Jones, a resident of Texas, receives a call from his investment representative, Bob, in New York. Bob recommends that Mr. Jones purchase 500 shares of XYZ based on his company's research and in line with Mr. Jones's investment objectives. Mr. Jones accepts the recommendation and purchases the 500 shares at the market.
>
> In this case, the securities administrators in both Texas and New York have jurisdiction over the transaction. The state securities administrator from Texas can review the transaction because the sale was directed and accepted in Texas. Additionally, the state securities administrator from New York may review the transaction because the transaction originated from the representative's office within the state.
>
> If in the above case Mr. Jones tells his representative that he'll think about it and then calls his representative in New York the next day from

his summer home in California and purchases XYZ, the transaction would be subject to the jurisdiction of three state securities administrators:

1. The administrator from New York—because that is where the sale originated
2. The administrator from Texas—because that is where the sale was directed
3. The administrator from California—because that is where the sale was accepted

The state securities administrator also has jurisdiction over offers of securities that:

- Originated within the administrator's state.
- Are directed into the administrator's state.

An offer is considered to have been made in the state in which it originated as well as the state to which it is directed.

If, in our example, Bob, the representative in New York, directs the offer of XYZ to Mr. Jones in Texas, and Mr. Jones elects not to purchase the stock, the offer would be subject to the jurisdiction of the securities administrators in both New York and Texas. The state securities administrator in New York would have jurisdiction because that is where the representative was sitting when he made the offer. The administrator in Texas would have jurisdiction because that is where the offer was directed.

An offer or sale of a security that may be converted or exchanged into another security also constitutes an offer or sale of the security into which the original security may be converted.

The state securities administrator may:

- Investigate securities-related business within state borders.
- Issue subpoenas for people, books, and records from any state.
- Compel witnesses to testify.
- Issue cease and desist orders and seek injunctions.
- Deny, suspend, or revoke registrations, licenses, and exemptions.
- Adopt and amend rules.

The administrator may investigate complaints and alleged violations both in and out of the administrator's home state. The investigation may be conducted publicly or in private. During the course of an investigation, the administrator may subpoena people, books, and records from any state and may compel witnesses to testify under oath or to give a written sworn statement.

An individual brought before the administrator may not invoke his or her Fifth Amendment right against self-incrimination. The administrator may force the person to testify about the matter being investigated. However, a person who is forced to testify may not be prosecuted based on the testimony that he or she was compelled to offer. So a witness in this situation is given partial immunity.

If the administrator finds that a person has engaged in or is about to engage in any activity that would violate the USA, the administrator may issue a cease and desist order. A cease and desist order may be issued without a hearing. The administrator has the power to prevent violations before they take place. However, only a court of law has the authority to force compliance with the order and to prescribe penalties for violating the order.

RADIO, TELEVISION, AND NEWSPAPER DISTRIBUTION

An advertisement, offer, or solicitation will not have been made and will be outside the jurisdiction of a state securities administrator if the following conditions are met:

- The television broadcast originated outside the administrator's state.
- The radio broadcast originated outside the administrator's state.
- The newspaper or periodical was published outside the administrator's state.
- The newspaper or periodical was published inside the state but two thirds of its circulation is outside of the state of publication.

In the last case the circulation numbers are based on the preceding year. If the conditions are met the state securities administrator in the state of publication will not have jurisdiction because the advertisement, offer, or solicitation is not deemed to be made in the state where the publication originated.

RIGHT OF RESCISSION

If the seller of a security determines that the sale has violated a provision of the USA, the seller may offer the affected parties rescission. All offers of recession must be in writing and include an agreement to repurchase the securities at the original purchase price and must include interest for the time period that the money was invested.

If the buyer does not accept the offer of rescission within 30 days, the seller has no further liability with regard to the sale of those securities, and the buyer forfeits the right to sue.

An investor's acknowledgment that a sale is in violation of the USA is never valid.

EXAMPLE   A customer with an investment objective of speculation convinces their representative to sell them an interest in a private placement that will pay the representative a commission and is in violation of the USA. The investor is a nonaccredited investor and signs a letter stating that they recognize that the investment is in violation of the USA and will not sue or otherwise hold the representative or their firm responsible for any losses.

This acknowledgment by the client is neither valid nor enforceable and in no way protects the representative or the firm.

STATUTE OF LIMITATIONS

If a buyer of a security finds that the sale of the security violates any of the provisions of the USA, the purchaser has two years from the discovery of the violation or three years from the purchase date, whichever comes first, to take action.

CHAPTER 6

Pretest

THE STATE SECURITIES ADMINISTRATOR AND THE UNIFORM SECURITIES ACT

1. An administrator may require all of the following, EXCEPT:
   a. securities to be sold under a specific subscription form.
   b. an agent to take an oral exam.
   c. an issuer to file monthly financial reports.
   d. a specimen of the security.

2. A recent college graduate has just passed the Series 63 exam. The state securities administrator may deny the person registration based solely on:
   I. Lack of experience
   II. Public interest
   III. Lack of training
   IV. A felony conviction two years prior to the application for registration
   a. I and III
   b. III and IV
   c. I, II, and III
   d. II, III, and IV

3. A New York agent calls a customer who is a New Jersey resident vacationing in Florida at his hotel. The representative recommends that the client purchase 1,000 shares of ABC. The customer informs the representative that he will call him when he returns to New Jersey the following morning. On his return, the customer calls his representative and elects to purchase the 1,000 shares of ABC. Which state administrator has jurisdiction over this transaction?
   a. New York and Florida only
   b. New Jersey and New York only
   c. New York, New Jersey, and Florida
   d. New York only

4. A state securities administrator takes action against the principal of a firm for failing to supervise the actions of one of the firm's agents. Which of the following is true?
   I. The administrator may take action against the firm's registration.
   II. The administrator may not take action against the firm's registration.
   III. The agent's registration may be subject to action by the administrator.
   IV. Because the administrator has taken action against the supervisor, the administrator may not take action against the agent.
   a. I and II
   b. I and III
   c. II and III
   d. II and IV

5. A state securities administrator has sent a notice of its intention to revoke a firm's registration. The firm requests a hearing in writing. The hearing will be held within:
   a. 30 days.
   b. 15 days.
   c. 45 days.
   d. 60 days.

CHAPTER 6 Pretest   **115**

6. Which of the following is true regarding actions taken by an administrator?
   I. An administrator may issue subpoenas.
   II. An administrator may suspend a pending registration.
   III. An administrator issues a stop order without a hearing.
   IV. An individual who displays contempt for the administrator's order may be found in contempt of court.
   a. I and II
   b. II and IV
   c. II, III, and IV
   d. I, II, III, and IV

7. An administrator may do all of the following, EXCEPT:
   a. require the production of documents.
   b. administer oaths.
   c. compel testimony.
   d. order injunctions.

8. The Uniform Securities Act was designed to be enforced by which of the following?
   a. The SEC
   b. FINRA
   c. The states
   d. The federal government

9. Which of the following are true with regard to an investor's right of rescission?
   I. The investor has 30 days to accept the offer.
   II. It may be offered verbally.
   III. It must include an offer to pay interest.
   IV. The investor may receive punitive damages.
   a. I and II
   b. I and III
   c. I, II, and IV
   d. I, II, III, and IV

10. An agent who willfully violates the antifraud provision of the USA may be subject to which of the following?

   I. Three years in prison
   II. A $5,000 fine
   III. Five years in prison
   IV. A $10,000 fine

   a. I and II
   b. II only
   c. III and IV
   d. IV only

11. A client who determines that his firm has violated the USA by selling him certain securities has how long to take action against the firm under the USA?

   a. Six years
   b. Two years from the discovery or three years from the triggering event, whichever occurs first
   c. Five years
   d. There is no statute of limitations for violations of the USA

12. Which of the following is NOT a violation of the USA?

   a. Buying warrants and selling the issuer's common stock short
   b. Making market predictions
   c. Telling a customer that she cannot lose money by purchasing Treasury bonds because the principal is guaranteed by the U.S. government
   d. Printing "FINRA" in large letters on the firm's business card

13. Which of the following is a violation of the USA?

   a. Cold calling someone in a neighboring state
   b. Explaining to a customer that securities listed on the NYSE are safer than nonlisted securities
   c. Mailing 150 form letters to potential customers
   d. Failing to withhold capital gains taxes on the sale of a security

14. Which of the following is NOT a valid reason to deny the registration of an agent?
    a. The agent is being taken to arbitration by a number of clients for allegedly mishandling their accounts.
    b. The agent has a securities-related misdemeanor.
    c. The agent was convicted of fraud 8 years ago.
    d. It's solely deemed to be in the public's best interest.

15. A client who takes action against an investment adviser is entitled to all of the following under the USA, EXCEPT:
    a. reimbursement of fees.
    b. attorney's fees.
    c. treble damages.
    d. interest on money.

16. An agent has displayed a pattern of abusive activity. The administrator may take action against which of the following?
    I. The agent
    II. The principal of the firm
    III. The firm
    IV. Industry regulators for failing to supervise the firm
    a. I only
    b. I and III
    c. I, II, and III
    d. I, II, III, and IV

17. A customer who has rejected a broker dealer's offer of rescission may do which of the following under the USA?
    a. Reserve the right to accept the offer at a later date
    b. Sue the firm in court
    c. Take the firm to arbitration
    d. The customer has given up his or her rights of recovery

18. Which of the following is NOT a reason a state securities administrator may take action against an issuer?
    a. The promoter's fees are excessive.
    b. The registration statement is incomplete.
    c. The prospects for the issuer's industry are not strong.
    d. The issuer has relied on an exemption from registration based on a misleading application.

19. A broker dealer has withdrawn its state registration. The broker dealer's request to withdraw its registration will become effective in:
    a. 45 days.
    b. 30 days.
    c. 60 days.
    d. 90 days.

20. An offer of securities is subject to the jurisdiction of all of the following state securities administrators, EXCEPT:
    a. the state where the offer originated.
    b. the state where the issuer is headquartered.
    c. the state were the offer was directed.
    d. the state where the offer was accepted.

Answer Keys

CHAPTER 2: DEFINITION OF TERMS

1. (C) A minor is not considered a person because a minor may not enter into a legally binding contract.

2. (C) The pledge of securities as collateral for a margin loan is not considered a sale. All of the other choices constitute a sale, including a bonus security attached to another security, such as a warrant.

3. (D) A qualified purchaser must have at least $5,000,000 in assets. A family-owned business with $5,000,000 in investments is also a qualified purchaser.

4. (C) All of the choices listed are institutional investors except an employee benefit plan with $800,000 in assets. In order for the plan to be an institutional investor, it must have more than $10,000,000 in assets.

5. (B) A trust indenture is the contract between a corporate issuer of debt securities and a trustee. It is not a security.

6. (D) A gift of assessable stock is considered to be a sale. Assessable stock can require the owner to make additional payments.

7. (A) The publisher of a market report that charges a fee in excess of $200 per year based on market developments is an investment adviser.

8. (D) A family-owned business with at least $5,000,000 is a qualified purchaser.

9. (B) XYZ is a federally covered security and is given an exemption from state registration because it trades on a U.S. exchange.

10. (D) An interest in any of the items listed is a security.

11. (B) Only the company and the publisher of the market letter are investment advisers. Individuals are investment adviser representatives.
12. (D) The promise of a profit is not one of the requirements of the Howey test.
13. (D) A broker is a "person" that executes an order for its own account or for the accounts of others.
14. (D) An offer of securities is made through a prospectus.
15. (C) A corporation that issues securities or simply proposes to issue securities is considered an issuer.
16. (D) An individual representing an out-of-state broker dealer is required to register as an agent.
17. (A) A broker dealer with no office in the state that only conducts business with customers who do not reside in that state or who are in that state for less than 30 days and an out-of-state broker dealer that only conducts business with other broker dealers are not considered broker dealers in that state.
18. (D) Nasdaq OTCBB stocks are not a federally covered security. Only Nasdaq Global and capital market securities are given the federally covered exemption.
19. (C) A guarantee of interest or principal may be issued by all of those listed except an investment adviser.
20. (C) An offer has been made when a representative has made a recommendation.

CHAPTER 3: REGISTRATION OF BROKER DEALERS, INVESTMENT ADVISERS, AND AGENTS

1. (D) A broker dealer may not employ a person as an agent unless that person is duly registered.
2. (C) A broker dealer that meets the SEC's net capital requirement is exempt from the requirement.
3. (C) An investment adviser is limited to giving advice to five clients or fewer during a 12-month period under the de minimis exemption.
4. (D) All of the partners must register because all of them act in a sales capacity by managing portfolios at the time the firm initially registered. Partners who do not act in a sales capacity are not required to register.

5. (C) The pension consultant with $300,000,000 in assets must register with the SEC. All of the others are exempt unless they receive a specific fee for the advice.

6. (C) An investment adviser with between $100,000,000 and $110,000,000 may select either federal or state registration, depending on the prospects for receiving additional funds.

7. (D) At the time a client enters into a new advisory relationship all of the choices must be disclosed except the representative's compensation.

8. (C) An agent is exempt from registration if the agent represents an exempt issuer. A Canadian corporation is not an exempt issuer.

9. (D) The adviser whose assets have fallen to less than $90,000,000 must withdraw its federal registration.

10. (D) When an agent changes employment, the old employer, the new employer, and the agent all must notify the administrator.

11. (C) A broker dealer may also be registered as an investment adviser and may be a corporation or an individual.

12. (A) An investment adviser must keep books and records for five years, but two years readily accessible.

13. (C) A Canadian broker dealer in good standing with a Canadian securities regulator can register through a simplified registration process.

14. (B) An agent is not required to meet any financial solvency requirements.

15. (C) An investment adviser who does not have custody of client funds is not subject to the $35,000 requirement.

16. (C) The investment adviser must register in this case. An exemption is given to advisers who have given advice to five or fewer individuals in 12 months.

17. (A) Investors who open wrap accounts will be charged one fee for advice and execution. The investor must receive Schedule H at the time the account is opened.

18. (A) All registrations expire on December 31.

CHAPTER 4: SECURITIES REGISTRATION, EXEMPT SECURITIES, AND EXEMPT TRANSACTIONS

1. (C) This is an example of an exempt transaction. All transactions with financial institutions are exempt regardless of the security involved.

2. (B) A registered representative may sell an unregistered nonexempt security through a private placement.
3. (C) All unsolicited orders are exempt transactions. An unsolicited order is placed by the customer without any advice from the representative.
4. (B) Commercial paper must be issued in denominations exceeding $50,000 with a maturity of less than 270 days.
5. (C) These are examples of isolated nonissuer transactions.
6. (C) Securities given a federally covered exemption are exempt from state registration.
7. (A) Transactions with wealthy investors are not exempt transactions.
8. (D) A security listed on a foreign exchange is not an exempt security.
9. (D) A state registration becomes effective after 20 days provided no stop order has been issued. A securities' state registration may not become effective before its federal registration.
10. (B) A private placement may be sold to no more than 10 nonaccredited investors in a 12-month period under the Uniform Securities Act.
11. (B) State registration through coordination becomes effective at the same time as the federal registration.
12. (C) A recommendation to an investor involving a NYSE-listed security is not an exempt transaction.
13. (A) A security is not registered by application. Only an agent or a firm will file an application for registration
14. (C) A federally covered security is not required to register at the state level.
15. (A) Political subdivisions of foreign countries (except Canada) are not given an exemption from registration.
16. (C) A security whose registration statement has already become effective with the SEC would most likely register through notice filing.
17. (B) An isolated nonissuer transaction must be executed through a broker dealer or an investment adviser.
18. (C) A transaction with a trust administrator is an exempt transaction.

CHAPTER 5: PROFESSIONAL CONDUCT AND PROHIBITED AND FRAUDULENT ACTIONS

1. (C) It is sometimes reasonable to charge a larger than ordinary commission as long as it is disclosed to the customer.

2. **(B)** The spouse of a client may not enter an order for the client's account unless they are an owner of the account or have signed trading authorization.

3. **(B)** This is a violation known as painting the tape. The increased activity is used to attract new buyers.

4. **(B)** This is a violation. Any offer of free services must be totally free with no strings attached.

5. **(D)** A representative is not required to do anything in this case. If the client puts the complaint in writing, then the representative must inform the principal.

6. **(B)** This is permitted for joint accounts approved by the firm.

7. **(A)** An agent may not make blanket recommendations, regardless of the security involved.

8. **(C)** This is a violation, since it is unreasonable for an agent to state that they will "constantly" monitor a client's account.

9. **(B)** This is an acceptable practice since all exempt securities are unregistered. A security that is "exempt" is exempt from registration and is thereby unregistered.

10. **(D)** An agent who recommends a security to a client that the firm does not conduct business in without the firm's knowledge has committed a violation known as selling away.

11. **(B)** The representative should only accept the order for the client's account. Once the contribution has been made to the nonworking spouse's account, it becomes the property of that individual.

12. **(D)** The representative may do all of the things listed except tell their clients to sell.

13. **(D)** The agent has misrepresented the risk, which is always a violation, and the agent could be held liable.

14. **(C)** A customer who has given a representative discretionary authority is bound by the decisions of the representative.

15. **(B)** A market maker may sell a security to a customer at the offer after just having purchased it at the bid.

16. **(C)** The agent must disclose the relationship to the customer prior to executing the order.

17. **(B)** This is a violation. A representative must always follow a client's instructions.

18. **(B)** The representative must always disclose material facts.

19. (C) A representative may not state that a security's price will go up nor can they repeat rumors.
20. (A) A representative may only accept the order that allows them to determine the best time and price for the transaction.

CHAPTER 6: THE STATE SECURITIES ADMINISTRATOR AND THE UNIFORM SECURITIES ACT

1. (C) A state securities administrator may not require an issuer to file reports more than quarterly.
2. (B) An agent may be denied a registration based on lack of training or a criminal record. An agent may not be denied a registration solely based on the public interest or lack of experience.
3. (C) All three administrators would have jurisdiction over this transaction: New York, because that is where the offer originated; Florida, because that is where the offer was directed; and New Jersey, because that is where the client accepted the offer.
4. (B) The administrator may take action against both the firm and the agent.
5. (B) The administrator must hold a hearing within 15 days of receiving a written request.
6. (D) An administrator may do all of the choices listed and an individual may be found in contempt of court for displaying contumacy.
7. (D) An administrator may not order an injunction. Only a court may order an injunction. The administrator may ask a court for an injunction, but the court must order it.
8. (C) The Uniform Securities Act was designed to be enforced and administered by the state.
9. (B) If an investor has been offered rescission, the offer must be accepted within 30 days and it must pay the investor interest for the time that the money was invested.
10. (A) An individual who willfully violates the Uniform Securities Act may be fined $5,000, up to three years in prison, or both.
11. (B) An investor who discovers a violation has two years from the discovery or three years from the triggering event, whichever occurs first, to take action.

12. **(A)** All of the choices listed are violations except buying warrants and selling the issuer's common stock short. This is an example of an arbitrage transaction.

13. **(B)** Implying that one security is safer than another due to its exchange listing is a violation.

14. **(D)** An agent may not be denied a registration solely on the basis of the public interest.

15. **(C)** A client is not entitled to treble damages.

16. **(C)** It is highly unlikely that an administrator would try to take action against another regulator.

17. **(D)** A customer who has rejected an offer of rescission has forfeited his rights of recovery.

18. **(C)** An administrator may not take action against an issuer's registration because the administrator does not think that the industry has good prospects for the issuer.

19. **(B)** The withdrawal of a registration will become effective after 30 days, as long as no action is being taken against the broker dealer.

20. **(B)** An offer of securities is not subject to the jurisdiction of the administrator in the state where the issuer is headquartered.

Glossary of Exam Terms

A

AAA/Aaa	The highest investment-grade rating for bond issuers awarded by Standard & Poor's and Moody's ratings agencies.
acceptance waiver and consent (AWAC)	A process used when a respondent does not contest an allegation made by FINRA. The respondent accepts the findings without admitting any wrongdoing and agrees to accept any penalty for the violation.
account executive (AE)	An individual who is duly licensed to represent a broker dealer in securities transactions or investment banking business. Also known as a registered representative.
accredited investor	Any individual or institution that meets one or more of the following: (1) a net worth exceeding $1 million, excluding the primary residence, or (2) is single and has an annual income of $200,000 or more or $300,000 jointly with a spouse.
accretion	An accounting method used to step up an investor's cost base for a bond purchased at a discount.
accrued interest	The portion of a debt securities future interest payment that has been earned by the seller of the security. The purchaser must pay this amount of accrued interest to the seller at the time of the transaction's settlement. Interest accrues from the date of the last interest payment date up to, but not including, the transaction's settlement date.
accumulation stage	The period during which an annuitant is making contributions to an annuity contract.
accumulation unit	A measure used to determine the annuitant's proportional ownership interest in the insurance company's separate account during the accumulation stage. During the accumulation stage, the number of accumulation units owned by the annuitant changes and their value varies.
acid-test ratio	A measure of corporate liquidity found by subtracting inventory from current assets and dividing the result by the current liabilities.
ACT	*See* Automated Comparison Transaction (ACT) service.
ad valorem tax	A tax based on the value of the subject property.

adjusted basis	The value assigned to an asset after all deductions or additions for improvements have been taken into consideration.
adjusted gross income (AGI)	An accounting measure employed by the IRS to help determine tax liability. AGI = earned income + investment income (portfolio income) + capital gains + net passive income.
administrator	(1) An individual authorized to oversee the liquidation of an intestate decedent's estate. (2) An individual or agency that administers securities' laws within a state.
ADR/ADS	See American depositary receipt (ADR).
advance/decline line	Measures the health of the overall market by calculating advancing issues and subtracting the number of declining issues.
advance refunding	The early refinancing of municipal securities. A new issue of bonds is sold to retire the old issue at its first available call date or maturity.
advertisement	Any material that is distributed by a broker dealer or issuer for the purpose of increasing business or public awareness for the firm or issuer. The broker dealer or issuer must distribute advertisements to an audience that is not controlled. Advertisements are distributed through any of the following: newspapers/magazines, radio, TV, billboards, telephone.
affiliate	An individual who owns 10% or more of the company's voting stock. In the case of a direct participation program (DPP), this is anyone who controls the partnership or is controlled by the partnership.
agency issue	A debt security issued by any authorized entity of the U.S. government. The debt security is an obligation of the issuing entity, not an obligation of the U.S. government (with the exception of Ginnie Mae and the Federal Import Export Bank issues).
agency transaction	A transaction made by a firm for the benefit of a customer. The firm merely executes a customer's order and charges a fee for the service, which is known as a commission.
agent	A firm or an individual who executes securities transactions for customers and charges a service fee known as a commission. Also known as a broker.
aggregate indebtedness	The total amount of the firm's customer-related debts.
allied member	An owner-director or 5% owner of an NYSE member firm. Allied members may not trade on the floor.
all-or-none (AON) order	A non-time-sensitive order that stipulates that the customer wants to buy or sell all of the securities in the order.
all-or-none underwriting	A type of underwriting that states that the issuer wants to sell all of the securities being offered or none of the securities being offered. The proceeds from the issue will be held in escrow until all securities are sold.
alpha	A measure of the projected change in the security's price as a result of fundamental factors relating only to that company.
alternative minimum tax (AMT)	A method used to calculate the tax liability for some high-income earners that adds back the deductions taken for certain tax preference items.

AMBAC Indemnity Corporation	Insures the interest and principal payments for municipal bonds.
American depositary receipt (ADR)/American depositary security (ADS)	A receipt representing the beneficial ownership of foreign securities being held in trust overseas by a foreign branch of a U.S. bank. ADRs/ADSs facilitate the trading and ownership of foreign securities and trade in the United States on an exchange or in the over-the-counter markets.
American Stock Exchange (AMEX)	An exchange located in New York using the dual-auction method and specialist system to facilitate trading in stocks, options, exchange-traded funds, and portfolios. AMEX was acquired by the NYSE Euronext and is now part of NYSE Alternext.
amortization	An accounting method that reduces the value of an asset over its projected useful life. Also the way that loan principal is systematically paid off over the life of a loan.
annual compliance review	All firms must hold at least one compliance meeting per year with all of its agents.
annuitant	An individual who receives scheduled payments from an annuity contract.
annuitize	A process by which an individual converts from the accumulation stage to the payout stage of an annuity contract. This is accomplished by exchanging accumulation units for annuity units. Once a payout option is selected, it cannot be changed.
annuity	A contract between an individual and an insurance company that is designed to provide the annuitant with lifetime income in exchange for either a lump sum or periodic deposits into the contract.
annuity unit	An accounting measure used to determine an individual's proportionate ownership of the separate account during the payout stage of the contract. The number of annuity units owned by an individual remains constant, and their value, which may vary, is used to determine the amount of the individual's annuity payment.
appreciation	An asset's increase in value over time.
arbitrage	An investment strategy used to profit from market inefficiencies.
arbitration	A forum provided by both the NYSE and FINRA to resolve disputes between two parties. Only a public customer may not be forced to settle a dispute through arbitration. The public customer must agree to arbitration in writing. All industry participants must settle disputes through arbitration.
ask	See offer.
assessed value	A base value assigned to property for the purpose of determining tax liability.
assessment	An additional amount of taxes due as a result of a municipal project that the homeowner benefits from. Also an additional call for capital by a direct participation program.
asset	Anything of value owned by an individual or a corporation.
asset allocation fund	A mutual fund that spreads its investments among different asset classes (i.e., stocks, bonds, and other investments) based on a predetermined formula.
assignee	A person to whom the ownership of an asset is being transferred.

assignment	(1) The transfer of ownership or rights through a signature. (2) The notification given to investors who are short an option that the option holder has exercised its right and they must now meet their obligations as detailed in the option contract.
associated person	Any individual under the control of a broker dealer, issuer, or bank, including employees, officers, and directors, as well as those individuals who control or have common control of a broker dealer, issuer, or bank.
assumed interest rate (AIR)	(1) A benchmark used to determine the minimum rate of return that must be realized by a variable annuity's separate account during the payout phase in order to keep the annuitant's payments consistent. (2) In the case of a variable life insurance policy, the minimum rate of return that must be achieved in order to maintain the policy's variable death benefit.
at-the-close order	An order that stipulates that the security is to be bought or sold only at the close of the market, or as close to the close as Is reasonable, or not at all.
at the money	A term used to describe an option when the underlying security price is equal to the exercise price of the option.
at-the-opening order	An order that stipulates that the security is to be bought or sold only at the opening of the market, or as close to the opening as is reasonable, or not at all.
auction market	The method of trading employed by stock exchanges that allows buyers and sellers to compete with one another in a centralized location.
authorized stock	The maximum number of shares that a corporation can sell in an effort to raise capital. The number of authorized shares may only be changed by a vote of the shareholders.
Automated Comparison Transaction (ACT) service	ACT is the service that clears and locks Nasdaq trades.
average cost	A method used to determine the cost of an investment for an investor who has made multiple purchases of the same security at different times and prices. An investor's average cost may be used to determine a cost base for tax purposes or to evaluate the profitability of an investment program, such as dollar-cost averaging. Average cost is determined by dividing the total dollars invested by the number of shares purchased.
average price	A method used to determine the average price paid by an investor for a security that has been purchased at different times and prices, such as through dollar-cost averaging. An investor's average price is determined by dividing the total of the purchase prices by the number of purchases.

B

BBB/Baa	The lowest ratings assigned by Standard & Poor's and Moody's for debt in the investment-grade category.
back-end load	A mutual fund sales charge that is assessed upon the redemption of the shares. The amount of the sales charge to be assessed upon redemption decreases the longer the shares are held. Also known as a contingent deferred sales charge.

backing away	The failure of an over-the-counter market maker to honor firm quotes. It is a violation of FINRA rules.
balanced fund	A mutual fund whose investment policy requires that the portfolio's holdings are diversified among asset classes and invested in common and preferred stock, bonds, and other debt instruments. The exact asset distribution among the asset classes will be predetermined by a set formula that is designed to balance out the investment return of the fund.
balance of payments	The net balance of all international transactions for a country in a given time.
balance of trade	The net flow of goods into or out of a country for a given period. Net exports result in a surplus or credit; net exports result in a deficit or net debit.
balance sheet	A corporate report that shows a company's financial condition at the time the balance sheet was created.
balance sheet equation	Assets = liabilities + shareholders equity.
balloon maturity	A bond maturity schedule that requires the largest portion of the principal to be repaid on the last maturity date.
bankers' acceptance (BA)	A letter of credit that facilitates foreign trade. BAs are traded in the money market and have a maximum maturity of 270 days.
basis	The cost that is assigned to an asset.
basis book	A table used to calculate bond prices for bonds quoted on a yield basis and to calculate yields for bonds quoted on a price basis.
basis point	Measures a bond's yield; 1 basis point is equal to 1/100 of 1%.
basis quote	A bond quote based on the bond's yield.
bearer bond	A bond that is issued without the owner's name being registered on the bond certificate or the books of the issuer. Whoever has possession of (bears) the certificate is deemed to be the rightful owner.
bearish	An investor's belief that prices will decline.
bear market	A market condition that is characterized by continuing falling prices and a series of lower lows in overall prices.
best efforts underwriting	A type of underwriting that does not guarantee the issuer that any of its securities will be sold.
beta	A measure of a security's or portfolio's volatility relative to the market as a whole. A security or portfolio whose beta is greater than 1 will experience a greater change in price than overall market prices. A security or portfolio with a beta of less than 1 will experience a price change that is less than the price changes realized by the market as a whole.
bid	A price that an investor or broker dealer is willing to pay for a security. It is also a price at which an investor may sell a security immediately and the price at which a market maker will buy a security.
blind pool	A type of direct participation program where less than 75% of the assets to be acquired have been identified.
block trade	A trade involving 10,000 shares or market value of over $200,000.

blotter	A daily record of broker dealer transactions.
blue chip stock	Stock of a company whose earnings and dividends are stable regardless of the economy.
blue sky	A term used to describe the state registration process for a security offering.
blue-sky laws	Term used to describe the state-based laws enacted under the Uniform Securities Act.
board broker	*See* order book official.
board of directors	A group of directors elected by the stockholders of a corporation to appoint and oversee corporate management.
Board of Governors	The governing body of FINRA. The board is made up of 27 members elected by FINRA's membership and the board itself.
bona fide quote	*See* firm quote.
bond	The legal obligation of a corporation or government to repay the principal amount of debt along with interest at a predetermined schedule.
bond anticipation note	Short-term municipal financing sold in anticipation of long-term financing.
bond buyer indexes	A group of yield-based municipal bond indexes published daily in the *Daily Bond Buyer*.
bond counsel	An attorney for the issuer of municipal securities who renders the legal opinion.
bond fund	A fund whose portfolio is made up of debt instruments issued by corporations, governments, and/or their agencies. The fund's investment objective is usually current income.
bond interest coverage ratio	A measure of the issuer's liquidity. It demonstrates how many times the issuer's earnings will cover its bond interest expense.
bond quotes	Corporate and government bond quotes are based on a percentage of par. Municipal bonds are usually quoted on a yield-to-maturity basis.
bond rating	A rating that assesses the financial soundness of issuers and their ability to make interest and principal payments in a timely manner. Standard & Poor's and Moody's are the two largest ratings agencies. Issuers must request and pay for the service to rate their bonds.
bond ratio	A measure used to determine how much of the corporation's capitalization was obtained through the issuance of bonds.
bond swap	The sale and purchase of two different bonds to allow the investor to claim a loss on the bond being sold without violating wash sale rules.
book entry	Securities that are issued in book entry form do not offer any physical certificates as evidence of ownership. The owner's name is registered on the books of the issuer, and the only evidence of ownership is the trade confirmation.
book value	A corporation's book value is the theoretical liquidation value of the company. Book value is in theory what someone would be willing to pay for the entire company.
book value per bond	A measure used to determine the amount of the corporation's tangible value for each bond issued.

book value per share	Used to determine the tangible value of each common share. It is found by subtracting intangible assets and the par value of preferred stock from the corporation's total net worth and dividing that figure by the number of common shares outstanding.
branch office	A branch office of a member firm is required to display the name of the member firm and is any office in which the member conducts securities business outside of its main office.
breadth	A measure of the broad market's health. It measures how many stocks are increasing and how many are declining.
breakdown	A technical term used to describe the price action of a security when it falls below support to a lower level and into a new trading range.
breakeven point	The point at which the value of a security or portfolio is exactly equal to the investor's cost for that security or portfolio.
breakout	A technical term used to describe the price action of a security when it increases past resistance to a higher level and into a new trading range.
breakpoint sale	The practice of selling mutual fund shares in dollar amounts that are just below the point where an investor would be entitled to a sales charge reduction. A breakpoint sale is designed for the purpose of trying to earn a larger commission. This is a violation of the Rules of Fair Practice and should never be done.
breakpoint schedule	A breakpoint schedule offers mutual fund investors reduced sales charges for larger dollar investments.
broad-based index	An index that represents a large cross-section of the market as a whole. The price movement of the index reflects the price movement of a large portion of the market, such as the S&P 500 or the Wilshire 5000.
broker	*See* agent.
broker dealer	A person or firm who buys and sells securities for its own account and for the accounts of others. When acting as a broker or agent for a customer, the broker dealer is merely executing the customer's orders and charging the customer a fee known as a commission. When acting as a dealer or principal, the broker dealer is trading for its own account and participating in the customer's transaction by taking the other side of the trade and charging the customer a markup or markdown. A firm also is acting as a principal or dealer when it is trading for its own account and making markets in OTC securities.
broker's broker	(1) A municipal bond dealer who specializes in executing orders for other dealers who are not active in the municipal bond market. (2) A specialist on the exchange executing orders for other members or an OTC market.
bullish	An investor who believes that the price of a security or prices as a whole will rise is said to be bullish.
bull market	A market condition that is characterized by rising prices and a series of higher highs.
business cycle	The normal economic pattern that is characterized by four stages: expansion, peak, contraction, and trough. The business cycle constantly repeats itself and the economy is always in flux.
business day	The business day in the securities industry is defined as the time when the financial markets are open for trading.

buyer's option	A settlement option that allows the buyer to determine when the transaction will settle.
buy in	An order executed in the event of a customer's or firm's failure to deliver the securities it sold. The buyer repurchases the securities in the open market and charges the seller for any loss.
buying power	The amount of money available to buy securities.
buy stop order	A buy stop order is used to protect against a loss or to protect a profit on a short sale of stock.

C

call	(1) A type of option that gives the holder the right to purchase a specified amount of the underlying security at a stated price for a specified period of time. (2) The act of exercising a call option.
callable bond	A bond that may be called in or retired by the issuer prior to its maturity date.
callable preferred	A preferred share issued with a feature allowing the issuing corporation to retire it under certain conditions.
call date	A specific date after which the securities in question become callable by the issuer.
call feature	A condition attached to some bonds and preferred stocks that allows the issuer to call in or redeem the securities prior to their maturity date and according to certain conditions.
call price	The price that will be paid by the issuer to retire the callable securities in question. The call price is usually set at a price above the par value of the bond or preferred stock, which is the subject of the call.
call protection	A period of time, usually right after the securities' issuance, when the securities may not be called by the issuer. Call protection usually ranges from 5 to 10 years.
call provision	*See* call feature.
call risk	The risk borne by the owner of callable securities that may require that the investor accept a lower rate of return once the securities have been called. Callable bonds and preferred stock are more likely to be called when interest rates are low or are falling.
call spread	An option position consisting of one long and one short call on the same underlying security with different strike prices, expirations, or both.
call writer	An investor who has sold a call.
capital	Money and assets available to use in an attempt to earn more money or to accumulate more assets.
capital appreciation	An increase in an asset's value over time.
capital assets	Tangible assets, including securities, real estate, equipment, and other assets, owned for the long term.
capital gain	A profit realized on the sale of an asset at a price that exceeds its cost.

capitalization	The composition of a company's financial structure. It is the sum of paid-in capital + paid-in surplus + long-term debt + retained earnings.
capital loss	A loss realized on the sale of an asset at a price that is lower than its cost.
capital market	The securities markets that deal in equity and debt securities with more than 1 year to maturity.
capital risk	The risk that the value of an asset will decline and cause an investor to lose all or part of the invested capital.
capital stock	The sum of the par value of all of a corporation's outstanding common and preferred stock.
capital structure	*See* capitalization.
capital surplus	The amount of money received by an issuer in excess of the par value of the stock at the time of its initial sale to the public.
capped index option	An index option that trades like a spread and is automatically exercised if it goes 30 points in the money.
capping	A manipulative practice of selling stock to depress the price.
carried interest	A sharing arrangement for an oil and gas direct participation program where the general partner shares in the tangible drilling costs with the limited partners.
cash account	An account in which the investor must deposit the full purchase price of the securities by the fourth business day after the trade date. The investor is not required by industry regulations to sign anything to open a cash account.
cash assets ratio	The most liquid measure of a company's solvency. The cash asset ratio is found by dividing cash and equivalents by current liabilities.
cash dividend	The distribution of corporate profits to shareholders of record. Cash dividends must be declared by the company's board of directors.
cash equivalent	Short-term liquid securities that can quickly be converted into cash. Money market instruments and funds are the most common examples.
cash flow	A company's cash flow equals net income plus depreciation.
cashiering department	The department in a brokerage firm that is responsible for the receipt and delivery of cash and securities.
cash management bill	Short-term federal financing issued in minimum denominations of $10 million.
cash settlement	A transaction that settles for cash requires the delivery of the securities from the seller as well as the delivery of cash from the buyer on the same day of the trade. A trade done for cash settles the same day.
catastrophe call	The redemption of a bond by an issuer due to the destruction of the facility that was financed by the issue. Issuers will carry insurance to cover such events and to pay off the bondholders.
certificate of deposit (CD)	An unsecured promissory note issued as evidence of ownership of a time deposit that has been guaranteed by the issuing bank.
certificates of accrual on Treasury securities	Zero-coupon bonds issued by brokerage firms and collateralized by Treasury securities.
change	The difference between the current price and the previous day's closing price.

Chicago Board of Trade (CBOT)	A commodity exchange that provides a marketplace for agricultural and financial futures.
Chicago Board Options Exchange (CBOE)	The premier option exchange in the United States for listed options.
Chinese wall	The physical separation that is required between investment banking and trading and retail divisions of a brokerage firm. Now known as a firewall.
churning	Executing transactions that are excessive in their frequency or size in light of the resources of the account for the purpose of generating commissions. Churning is a violation of the Rules of Fair Practice.
class A share	A mutual fund share that charges a front-end load.
class B share	A mutual fund share that charges a back-end load.
class C share	A mutual fund share that charges a level load.
class D share	A mutual fund share that charges a level load and a back-end load.
classical economics	A theory stating that the economy will do the best when the government does not interfere.
clearing firm	A firm that carries its customers' cash and securities and/or provides the service to customers of other firms.
clearinghouse	An agency that guarantees and settles futures and option transactions.
close	The last price at which a security traded for the day.
closed-end indenture	A bond indenture that will not allow additional bonds to be issued with the same claim on the issuer's assets.
closed-end investment company	A management company that issues a fixed number of shares to investors in a managed portfolio and whose shares are traded in the secondary market.
closing date	The date when sales of interest in a direct participation plan will cease.
closing purchase	An order executed to close out a short option position.
Code of Arbitration Procedure	The FINRA bylaw that provides for a forum for dispute resolution relating to industry matters. All industry participants must arbitrate in public and the customer must agree to arbitration in writing.
Code of Procedure	The FINRA bylaw that sets guidelines for the investigation of trade practice complaints and alleged rule violations.
coincident indicator	An economic indicator that moves simultaneously with the movement of the underlying economy.
collateral	Assets pledged to a lender. If the borrower defaults, the lender will take possession of the collateral.
collateral trust certificate	A bond backed by the pledge of securities the issuer owns in another entity.
collateralized mortgage obligation (CMO)	A corporate debt security that is secured by an underlying pool of mortgages.

collection ratio	A measure of a municipality's ability to collect the taxes it has assessed.
collect on delivery (COD)	A method of trade settlement that requires the physical delivery of the securities to receive payment.
combination	An option position with a call and put on the same underlying security with different strike prices and expiration months on both.
combination fund	A mutual fund that tries to achieve growth and current income by combining portfolios of common stock with portfolios of high-yielding equities.
combination preferred stock	A preferred share with multiple features, such as cumulative and participating.
combination privileges	A feature offered by a mutual fund family that allows an investor to combine two simultaneous purchases of different portfolios in order to receive a reduced sales charge on the total amount invested.
combined account	A margin account that contains both long and short positions.
commercial paper	Short-term unsecured promissory notes issued by large financially stable corporations to obtain short-term financing. Commercial paper does not pay interest and is issued at a discount from its face value. All commercial paper matures in 270 days or less and matures at its face value.
commingling	A FINRA violation resulting from the mixing of customer and firm assets in the same account.
commission	A fee charged by a broker or agent for executing a securities transaction.
commission house broker	A floor broker who executes orders for the firm's account and for the accounts of the firm's customers on an exchange.
common stock	A security that represents the ownership of a corporation. Common stockholders vote to elect the board of directors and to institute major corporate policies.
common stock ratio	A measure of how much of a company's capitalization was obtained through the sale of common stock. The ratio is found by summing the par value of the common stock, excess paid in capital, and retained earnings, and then dividing that number by the total capitalization.
competitive bid underwriting	A method of underwriter selection that solicits bids from multiple underwriters. The underwriter submitting the best terms will be awarded the issue.
compliance department	The department of a broker dealer that ensures that the firm adheres to industry rules and regulations.
concession	The amount of an underwriting discount that is allocated to a syndicate member or a selling group member for selling new securities.
conduct rules	The Rules of Fair Practice.
conduit theory	The IRS classification that allows a regulated investment company to avoid paying taxes on investment income it distributes to its shareholders.
confirmation	The receipt for a securities transaction that must be sent to all customers either on or before the completion of a transaction. The confirmation must show the trade date, settlement date, and total amount due to or from the customer. A transaction is considered to be complete on settlement date.

consolidated tape	The consolidated tape A displays transactions for NYSE securities that take place on the NYSE, all regional exchanges, and the third markets. The consolidated tape B reports transactions for $AMEX$ stocks that take place on the American Stock Exchange, all regional exchanges, and in the third market.
consolidation	A chart pattern that results from a narrowing of a security's trading range.
constant dollar plan	An investment plan designed to keep a specific amount of money invested in the market regardless of the market's condition. An investor will sell when the value of the account rises and buy when the value of the account falls.
constant ratio plan	An investment plan designed to keep the investor's portfolio invested at a constant ratio of equity and debt securities.
construction loan note	A short-term municipal note designed to provide financing for construction projects.
constructive receipt	The time when the IRS determines that the taxpayer has effectively received payment.
consumer price index (CPI)	A price-based index made up of a basket of goods and services that are used by consumers in their daily lives. An increase in the CPI indicates a rise in overall prices, while a decline in the index represents a fall in overall prices.
consumption	A term used to describe the purchase of newly produced household goods.
contemporaneous trader	A trader who enters an order on the other side of the market at the same time as a trader with inside information enters an order. Contemporaneous traders can sue traders who act on inside information to recover losses.
contingent deferred sales charge	*See* back-end load.
contraction	A period of declining economic output. Also known as a recession.
contractual plan	A mutual fund accumulation plan under which the investor agrees to contribute a fixed sum of money over time. If the investor does not complete or terminates the contract early, the investor may be subject to penalties.
control	The ability to influence the actions of an organization or individual.
control person	A director or officer of an issuer or broker dealer or a 10% stockholder of a corporation.
control stock	Stock that is acquired or owned by an officer, director, or person owning 10% or more of the outstanding stock of a company.
conversion price	The set price at which a convertible security may be exchanged for another security.
conversion privilege	The right offered to a mutual fund investor that allows the investor to move money between different portfolios offered by the same mutual fund family without paying another sales charge.
conversion ratio	The number of shares that can be received by the holder of a convertible security if it were converted into the underlying common stock.
convertible bond	A bond that may be converted or exchanged for common shares of the corporation at a predetermined price.
convertible preferred stock	A preferred stock that may be converted or exchanged for common shares of the corporation at a predetermined price.

cooling-off period	The period of time between the filing of a registration statement and its effective date. During this time, the SEC is reviewing the registration statement and no sales may take place. The cooling-off period is at least 20 days.
coordination	A method of securities registration during which a new issue is registered simultaneously at both the federal and state levels.
corporate account	An investment account for the benefit of a company that requires a corporate resolution listing the names of individuals who may transact business in the company's name.
corporate bond	A legally binding obligation of a corporation to repay a principal amount of debt along with interest at a predetermined rate and schedule.
corporation	A perpetual entity that survives after the death of its officers, directors, and stockholders. It is the most common form of business entity.
correspondent broker dealer	A broker dealer who introduces customer accounts to a clearing broker dealer.
cost basis	The cost of an asset, including any acquisition costs. It is used to determine capital gains and losses.
cost depletion	A method used to determine the tax deductions for investors in oil and gas programs.
cost of carry	All costs incurred by an investor for maintaining a position in a security, including margin interest and opportunity costs.
coterminous	Municipalities that share the same borders and have overlapping debt.
coupon bond	See bearer bond.
coupon yield	See nominal yield.
covenant	A promise made by an issuer of debt that describes the issuer's obligations and the bondholders' rights.
covered call	The sale of a call against a long position in the underlying security.
covered put	The sale of a put against a short position in the underlying security or against cash that will allow the person to purchase the security if the put is exercised.
CPI	See consumer price index (CPI).
credit agreement	The portion of the margin agreement that describes the terms and conditions under which credit will be extended to the customer.
credit balance	The cash balance in a customer's account.
credit department	See margin department.
credit risk	The risk that the issuer of debt securities will default on its obligation to pay interest or principal on a timely basis.
credit spread	An option position that results in a net premium or credit received by the investor from the simultaneous purchase and sale of two calls or two puts on the same security.
crossed market	A market condition that results when a broker enters a bid for a stock that exceeds the offering price for that stock. Also a condition that may result when a broker enters an offer that is lower than the bid price for that stock.

crossing stock	The pairing off of two offsetting customer orders by the same floor broker. The floor broker executing the cross must first show the order to the crowd for possible price improvement before crossing the orders.
crossover point	The point at which all tax credits have been used up by a limited partnership; results in a tax liability for the partners.
cum rights	A stock that is the subject of a rights offering and is trading with the rights attached to the common stock.
cumulative preferred stock	A preferred stock that entitles the holder to receive unpaid dividends prior to the payment of any dividends to common stockholders. Dividends that accumulate in arrears on cumulative issues are always the first dividends to be paid by a corporation.
cumulative voting	A method of voting that allows stockholders to cast all of their votes for one director or to distribute them among the candidates they wish to vote for. Cumulative voting favors smaller investors by allowing them to have a larger say in the election of the board of directors.
current assets	Cash, securities, accounts receivable, and other assets that can be converted into cash within 12 months.
current liabilities	Corporate obligations, including accounts payable, that must be paid within 12 months.
current market value (CMV)/current market price (CMP)	The present value of a marketable security or of a portfolio of marketable securities.
current ratio	A measure of a corporation's short-term liquidity found by dividing its current assets by its current liabilities.
current yield	A relationship between a securities annual income relative to its current market price. Determined by dividing annual income by the current market price.
CUSIP (Committee on Uniform Securities Identification Procedures)	A committee that assigns identification numbers to securities to help identify them.
custodial account	An account operated by a custodian for the benefit of a minor.
custodian	A party responsible for managing an account for another party. In acting as a custodian, the individual or corporation must adhere to the prudent man rule and only take such actions as a prudent person would do for him- or herself.
customer	Any individual or entity that maintains an account with a broker dealer.
customer agreement	An agreement signed by a customer at the time the account is opened, detailing the conditions of the customer's relationship with the firm. The customer agreement usually contains a predispute arbitration clause.
customer ledger	A ledger that lists all customer cash and margin accounts.
customer protection rule	Rule 15C3-3 requires that customer assets be kept segregated from the firm assets.
cyclical industry	An industry whose prospects fluctuate with the business cycle.

D

Daily Bond Buyer	A daily publication for the municipal securities industry that publishes information related to the municipal bond market and official notices of sales.
dated date	The day when interest starts to accrue for bonds.
dealer	(1) A person or firm who transacts securities business for its own account. (2) A brokerage firm acting as a principal when executing a customer's transaction or making markets over the counter.
dealer paper	Commercial paper sold to the public by a dealer, rather than placed with investors directly by the issuer.
debenture	An unsecured promissory note issued by a corporation backed only by the issuer's credit and promise to pay.
debit balance	The amount of money a customer owes a broker dealer.
debit spread	An option position that results in a net premium paid by the investor from the simultaneous purchase and sale of two calls or two puts on the same security.
debt securities	A security that represents a loan to the issuer. The owner of a debt security is a creditor of the issuing entity, be it a corporation or a government.
debt service	The scheduled interest payments and repayment of principal for debt securities.
debt service account	An account set up by a municipal issuer to pay the debt service of municipal revenue bonds.
debt service ratio	Indicates the issuer's ability to pay its interest and principal payments.
debt-to-equity ratio	A ratio that shows how highly leveraged the company is. It is found by dividing total long-term debt by total shareholder equity.
declaration date	The day chosen by the board of directors of a corporation to pay a dividend to shareholders.
deduction	An adjustment taken from gross income to reduce tax liability.
default	The failure of an issuer of debt securities to make interest and principal payments when they are due.
default risk	*See* credit risk.
defeasance	Results in the elimination of the issuer's debt obligations by issuing a new debt instrument to pay off the outstanding issue. The old issue is removed from the issuer's balance sheet and the proceeds of the new issue are placed in an escrow account to pay off the now-defeased issue.
defensive industry	A term used to describe a business whose economic prospects are independent from the business cycle. Pharmaceutical companies, utilities, and food producers are examples of defensive industries.
deferred annuity	A contract between an individual and an insurance company that delays payments to the annuitant until some future date.

deferred compensation plan	A contractual agreement between an employer and an employee under which the employee elects to defer receiving money owed until after retirement. Deferred compensation plans are typically unfunded, and the employee could lose all the money due under the agreement if the company goes out of business.
deficiency letter	A letter sent to a corporate issuer by the SEC, requesting additional information regarding the issuer's registration statement.
defined benefit plan	A qualified retirement plan established to provide a specific amount of retirement income for the plan participants. Unlike a defined contribution plan, the individual's retirement benefits are known prior to reaching retirement.
defined contribution plan	A qualified retirement plan that details the amount of money that the employer will contribute to the plan for the benefit of the employee. This amount is usually expressed as a percentage of the employee's gross annual income. The actual retirement benefits are not known until the employee reaches retirement, and the amount of the retirement benefit is a result of the contributions to the plan, along with the investment experience of the plan.
deflation	The economic condition that is characterized by a persistent decline in overall prices.
delivery	As used in the settlement process, results in the change of ownership of cash or securities.
delivery vs. payment	A type of settlement option that requires that the securities be physically received at the time payment is made.
delta	A measure of an option's price change in relation to a price change in the underlying security.
demand deposit	A deposit that a customer has with a bank or other financial institution that will allow the customer to withdraw the money at any time or on demand.
Department of Enforcement	The FINRA committee that has original jurisdiction over complaints and violations.
depletion	A tax deduction taken for the reduction in the amount of natural resources (e.g., gas, gold, oil) available to a business or partnership.
depreciation	A tax deduction taken for the reduction of value in a capital asset.
depreciation expense	A noncash expense that results in a reduction in taxable income.
depression	An economic condition that is characterized by a protracted decline in economic output and a rising level of unemployment.
derivative	A security that derives its value in whole or in part based on the price of another security. Options and futures are examples of derivative securities.
designated order	An order entered by an institution for a new issue of municipal bonds that states what firm and what agent is going to get the sales credit for the order.
devaluation	A significant fall in the value of a country's currency relative to other currencies. Devaluation could be the result of poor economic prospects in the home country. In extreme circumstances, it can be the result of government intervention.
developmental drilling program	An oil or gas program that drills for wells in areas of proven reserves.

developmental fee	A fee paid to organizers of a direct participation plan for the development of plans, obtaining financing or zoning authorizations, and other services.
diagonal spread	A spread that is created through the simultaneous purchase and sale of two calls or two puts on the same underlying security that differ in both strike price and expiration months.
dilution	A reduction in a stockholder's proportional ownership of a corporation as a result of the issuance of more shares. Earnings per share may also be diluted as a result of the issuance of additional shares.
direct debt	The total amount of a municipality's debt that has been issued by the municipality for its own benefit and for which the municipality is responsible to repay.
direct paper	Commercial paper sold to investors directly from the issuer without the use of a dealer.
direct participation program (DPP)	An entity that allows all taxable events to be passed through to investors, including limited partnerships and subchapter S corporations.
discount	The amount by which the price of a security is lower than its par value.
discount bond	A bond that is selling for a price that is lower than its par value.
discount rate	The rate that is charged to Federal Reserve member banks on loans directly from the Federal Reserve. This rate is largely symbolic, and member banks only borrow directly from the Federal Reserve as a last resort.
discretion	Authorization given to a firm or a representative to determine which securities are to be purchased and sold for the benefit of the customer without the customer's prior knowledge or approval.
discretionary account	An account where the owner has given the firm or the representative authority to transact business without the customer's prior knowledge or approval. All discretionary accounts must be approved and monitored closely by a principal of the firm.
disintermediation	The flow of money from traditional bank accounts to alternative higher yielding investments. This is more likely to occur as the Federal Reserve tightens monetary policy and interest rates rise.
disposable income	The sum of money an individual has left after paying taxes and required expenditures.
disproportional allocation	A method used by FINRA to determine if a free-riding violation has occurred with respect to a hot issuer. A firm is only allowed to sell up to 10% of a new issue to conditionally approved purchasers.
disproportionate sharing	An oil and gas sharing arrangement where the general partner pays a portion of the cost but receives a larger portion of the program's revenues.
distribution	Cash or property sent to shareholders or partners.
distribution stage	The period of time during which an annuitant is receiving payments from an annuity contract.
diversification	The distribution of investment capital among different investment choices. By purchasing several different investments, investors may be able to reduce their overall risk by minimizing the impact of any one security's adverse performance.

diversified fund/diversified management company	A mutual fund that distributes its investment capital among a wide variety of investments. In order for a mutual fund to market itself as a diversified mutual fund it must meet the 75-5-10 rule: 75% of the fund's assets must be invested in securities issued by other entities, no more than 5% of the fund's assets may be invested in any one issuer, and the fund may own no more than 10% of any one company's outstanding securities.
dividend	A distribution of corporate assets to shareholders. A dividend may be paid in cash, stock, or property or product.
dividend department	The department in a brokerage firm that is responsible for the collecting of dividends and crediting them to customer accounts.
dividend disbursement agent	An agent of the issuer who pays out the dividends to shareholders of record.
dividend payout ratio	The amount of a company's earnings that were paid out to shareholders relative to the total earnings that were available to be paid out to shareholders. It can be calculated by dividing dividends per share by earnings per share.
dividend yield	Also known as a stock's current yield. It is a relationship between the annual dividends paid to shareholders relative to the stock's current market price. To determine a stock's dividend yield, divide annual dividends by the current market price.
DJIA	See Dow Jones Industrial Average.
doctrine of mutual reciprocity	An agreement that the federal government would not tax interest income received by investors in municipal bonds and that reciprocally the states would not tax interest income received by investors in federal debt obligations.
dollar bonds	A term issue of municipal bonds that are quoted as a percentage of par rather than on a yield basis.
dollar-cost averaging	A strategy of investing a fixed sum of money on a regular basis into a fluctuating market price. Over time an investor should be able to achieve an average cost per share that is below the average price per share. Dollar-cost averaging is a popular investment strategy with mutual fund investors.
donor	A person who gives a gift of cash or securities to another person. Once the gift has been made, the donor no longer has any rights or claim to the security. All gifts to a minor are irrevocable.
do not reduce (DNR)	An order qualifier for an order placed under the market that stipulates that the price of the order is not to be reduced for the distribution of ordinary dividends.
don't know (DK)	A term used to describe a dealer's response to a confirmation for a trade they "don't know" doing.
Dow Jones Composite Average	A price weighted index composed of 65 stocks that is used as an indicator of market performance.
Dow Jones Industrial Average (DJIA)	A price weighted index composed of 30 industrial companies. The Dow Jones is the most widely quoted market index.
Dow Jones Transportation Average	A price weighted index composed of 20 transportation stocks.

Dow Jones Utility Average	An index composed of 15 utility stocks.
Dow theory	A theory that believes that the health of the market and the economy may be predicted by the performance of the Dow Jones Industrial Average.
dry hole	A term used to describe a nonproducing well.
dual-purpose fund	A mutual fund that offers two classes of shares to investors. One class is sold to investors seeking income and the other class is sold to investors seeking capital appreciation.

E

early withdrawal penalty	A penalty tax charged to an investor for withdrawing money from a qualified retirement plan prior to age 59-1/2, usually 10% on top of ordinary income taxes.
earned income	Money received by an individual in return for performing services.
earnings per share	The net amount of a corporation's earnings available to common shareholders divided by the number of common shares outstanding.
earnings per share fully diluted	The net amount of a corporation's earnings available to common shareholders after taking into consideration the potential conversion of all convertible securities.
eastern account	A type of syndicate account that requires all members to be responsible for their own allocation as well as for their proportional share of any member's unsold securities.
economic risk	The risk of loss of principal associated with the purchase of securities.
EE savings bonds	Nonmarketable U.S. government zero-coupon bonds that must be purchased from the government and redeemed to the government.
effective date	The day when a new issue's registration with the SEC becomes effective. Once the issue's registration statement has become effective, the securities may then be sold to investors.
efficient market theory	A theory that states that the market operates and processes information efficiently and prices in all information as soon as it becomes known.
Employee Retirement Income Security Act of 1974 (ERISA)	The legislation that governs the operation of private-sector pension plans. Corporate pension plans organized under ERISA guidelines qualify for beneficial tax treatment by the IRS.
endorsement	The signature on the back of a security that allows its ownership to be transferred.
EPS	*See* earnings per share.
equipment leasing limited partnership	A limited partnership that is organized to purchase equipment and lease it to corporations to earn lease income and to shelter passive income for investors.
equipment trust certificate	A bond backed by a pledge of large equipment, such as airplanes, railroad cars, and ships.

equity	A security that represents the ownership in a corporation. Both preferred and common equity holders have an ownership interest in the corporation.
equity financing	The sale of common or preferred equity by a corporation in an effort to raise capital.
equity option	An option to purchase or sell common stock.
ERISA	See Employee Retirement Income Security Act of 1974.
erroneous report	A report of an execution given in error to a client. The report is not binding on the firm or on the agent.
escrow agreement	Evidence of ownership of a security provided to a broker dealer as proof of ownership of the underlying security for covered call writers.
Eurobond	A bond issued in domestic currency of the issuer but sold outside of the issuer's country.
Eurodollar	A deposit held outside of the United States denominated in U.S. dollars.
Eurodollar bonds	A bond issued by a foreign issuer denominated in U.S. dollars.
Euroyen bonds	Bonds issued outside of Japan but denominated in yen.
excess equity (EE)	The value of an account's equity in excess of Regulation T.
exchange	A market, whether physical or electronic, that provides a forum for trading securities through a dual-auction process.
exchange distribution	A distribution of a large block of stock on the floor of the exchange that is crossed with offsetting orders.
exchange privilege	The right offered by many mutual funds that allows an investor to transfer or move money between different portfolios offered through the same fund company. An investor may redeem shares of the fund, which is being sold at the NAV, and purchase shares of the new portfolio at the NAV without paying another sales charge.
ex date/ex-dividend date	The first day when purchasers of a security will no longer be entitled to receive a previously declared dividend.
executor/executrix	An individual with the authority to manage the affairs of a decedent's estate.
exempt security	A security that is exempt from the registration requirements of the Securities Act of 1933.
exempt transaction	A transaction that is not subject to state registration.
exercise	An investor's election to take advantage of the rights offered through the terms of an option, a right, or a warrant.
exercise price	The price at which an option investor may purchase or sell a security. Also the price at which an investor may purchase a security through a warrant or right.
existing property program	A type of real estate direct participation program that purchases existing property for the established rental income.
expansion	A period marked by a general increase in business activity and an increase in gross domestic product.
expansionary policy	A monetary policy enacted through the Federal Reserve Board that in-creases money supply and reduces interest rates in an effort to stimulate the economy.

expense ratio	The amount of a mutual fund's expenses relative to its assets. The higher the expense ratio, the lower the investor's return. A mutual fund's expense ratio tells an investor how efficiently a mutual fund operates, not how profitable the mutual fund is.
expiration cycle	A 4-month cycle for option expiration: January, April, July, and October; February, May, August, and November; or March, June, September, and December.
expiration date	The date on which an option ceases to exist.
exploratory drilling program	A direct participation program that engages in the drilling for oil or gas in new areas seeking to find new wells.
exploratory well	Also known as wildcatting. The drilling for oil or gas in new areas in an effort to find new wells.
ex rights	The common stock subject to a rights offering trade without the rights attached.
ex rights date	The first day when the common stock is subject to a rights offering trade without the rights attached.
ex warrants	Common trading without the warrants attached.

F

face-amount certificate company (FAC)	A type of investment company that requires an investor to make fixed payments over time or to deposit a lump sum, and that will return to the investor a stated sum known as the face amount on a specific date.
face amount/face value	*See* par.
fail to deliver	An event where the broker on the sell side of the transaction fails to deliver the security.
fail to receive	An event where the broker on the buy side of the transaction fails to receive the security from the broker on the sell side.
Fannie Mae	*See* Federal National Mortgage Association.
Farm Credit Administrator	The agency that oversees all of the activities of the banks in the Federal Farm Credit System.
Federal Deposit Insurance Corporation (FDIC)	The government insurance agency that provides insurance for bank depositors in case of bank failure.
Federal Farm Credit System	An organization of banks that is designed to provide financing to farmers for mortgages, feed and grain, and equipment.
federal funds rate	The rate banks charge each other on overnight loans.
Federal Home Loan Mortgage Corporation (FHLMC; Freddie Mac)	A publicly traded for-profit corporation that provides liquidity to the secondary mortgage market by purchasing pools of mortgages from lenders and, in turn, issues mortgage-backed securities.

Federal Intermediate Credit Bank	Provides short-term financing to farmers for equipment.
Federal National Mortgage Association (FNMA; Fannie Mae)	A publicly traded for-profit corporation that provides liquidity to the secondary mortgage market by purchasing pools of mortgages and issuing mortgage-backed securities.
Federal Open Market Committee (FOMC)	The committee of the Federal Reserve Board that makes policy decisions relating to the nation's money supply.
Federal Reserve Board	A seven-member board that directs the policies of the Federal Reserve System. The members are appointed by the President and approved by Congress.
Federal Reserve System	The nation's central banking system, the purpose of which is to regulate money supply and the extension of credit. The Federal Reserve System is composed of 12 central banks and 24 regional banks, along with hundreds of national and state chartered banks.
fictitious quote	A quote that is not representative of an actual bid or offer for a security.
fidelity bond	A bond that must be posted by all broker dealers to ensure the public against employee dishonesty.
fill or kill (FK)	A type of order that requires that all of the securities in the order be purchased or sold immediately or not at all.
final prospectus	The official offering document for a security that contains the security's final offering price along with all information required by law for an investor to make an informed decision.
firm commitment underwriting	Guarantees the issuer all of the money right away. The underwriters purchase all of the securities from the issuer regardless of whether they can sell the securities to their customers.
firm quote	A quote displayed at which the dealer is obligated to buy or sell at least one round lot at the quoted price.
fiscal policy	Government policy designed to influence the economy through government tax and spending programs. The President and Congress control fiscal policy.
5% markup policy	FINRA's guideline that requires all prices paid by customers to be reasonably related to a security's market price. The 5% policy is a guideline, not a rule, and it does not apply to securities sold through a prospectus.
fixed annuity	An insurance contract where the insurance company guarantees fixed payments to the annuitant, usually until the annuitant's death.
fixed assets	Assets used by a corporation to conduct its business, such as plant and equipment.
flat	A term used to describe a bond that trades without accrued interest, such as a zero-coupon bond or a bond that is in default.
floor broker	An individual member of an exchange who may execute orders on the floor.
floor trader	Members of the exchange who trade for their own accounts. Members of the NYSE may not trade from the floor for their own accounts.
flow of funds	A schedule of expenses and interested parties that prioritizes how payments will be made from the revenue generated by a facility financed by a municipal revenue bond.

forced conversion	The calling in of convertible bonds at a price that is less than the market value of the underlying common stock into which the bonds may be converted.
foreign currency	Currency of another country.
foreign currency option	An option to purchase or sell a specified amount of another country's currency.
Form 10-K	An annual report filed by a corporation detailing its financial performance for the year.
Form 10-Q	A quarterly report filed by a corporation detailing its financial performance for the quarter.
form letter	A letter sent out by a brokerage firm or a registered representative to more than 25 people in a 90-day period. Form letters are subject to approval and recordkeeping requirements.
forward pricing	The way in which open-end mutual funds are valued for investors who wish to purchase or redeem shares of the fund. Mutual funds usually price their shares at the end of the business day. The price to be paid or received by the investor will be the price that is next calculated after the fund receives the order.
401K	A qualified retirement plan offered by an employer.
403B	A qualified retirement plan offered to teachers and employees of nonprofit organizations.
fourth market	A transaction between two large institutions without the use of a broker dealer.
fractional share	A portion of a whole share that represents ownership of an open-end mutual fund.
fraud	Any attempt to gain an unfair advantage over another party through the use of deception, concealment, or misrepresentation.
free credit balance	Cash reserves in a customer's account that have not been invested. Customers must be notified of their free credit balances at least quarterly.
free look	A privilege offered to purchasers of contractual plans and insurance policies that will allow the individual to cancel the contract within the free-look period, usually 45 days.
freeriding	The purchase and sale of a security without depositing the money required to cover the purchase price as required by Regulation T.
freeriding and withholding	The withholding of new issue securities offered by a broker dealer for the benefit of the brokerage firm or an employee.
front-end load	(1) A sales charge paid by investors in open-end mutual funds that is paid at the time of purchase. (2) A contractual plan that seeks to assess sales charges in the first years of the plan and may charge up to 50% of the first year's payments as sales charges.
frozen account	An account where the owner is required to deposit cash or securities up front, prior to any purchase or sale taking place. An account is usually frozen as a result of a customer's failure to pay or deliver securities.
full power of attorney	A type of discretionary authority that allows a third party to purchase and sell securities as well as to withdraw cash and securities without the owner's prior consent or knowledge. This type of authority is usually reserved to trustees and attorneys.

fully registered bonds	A type of bond issuance where the issuer has a complete record of the owners of the bonds and who is entitled to receive interest and principal payments. The owners of fully registered bonds are not required to clip coupons.
functional allocation	An arrangement for oil and gas programs where the general partner pays the tangible drilling costs and the limited partner absorbs the intangible drilling costs.
fundamental analyst	A method of valuing the company that takes into consideration the financial performance of the corporation, the value of its assets, and the quality of its management.
funded debt	Long-term debt obligations of corporations or municipalities.
fungible	Easily exchangeable items with the same conditions.

G

general account	An insurance company's account that holds the money and investments for fixed contracts and traditional life insurance policies.
general obligation bond	A municipal bond that is backed by the taxing power of the state or municipality.
general partner	The partner in a general partnership who manages the business and is responsible for any debt of the program.
general securities principal	An individual who has passed the Series 24 exam and may supervise the activities of the firm and its agents.
generic advertising	Advertising designed to promote name recognition for a firm and securities as investments, but does not recommend specific securities.
good 'til cancel (GTC)	An order that remains on the books until it is executed or canceled.
goodwill	An intangible asset of a corporation, such as its name recognition and reputation, that adds to its value.
Government National Mortgage Association (GNMA; Ginnie Mae)	A government corporation that provides liquidity to the mortgage markets by purchasing pools of mortgages that have been insured by the Federal Housing Administration and the Veterans Administration. Ginnie Mae issues pass-through certificates to investors backed by the pools of mortgages.
government security	A security that is an obligation of the U.S. government and that is backed by the full faith and credit of the U.S. government, such as Treasury bills, notes, and bonds.
grant anticipation note (GAN)	Short-term municipal financing issued in anticipation of receiving a grant from the federal government or one of its agencies.
greenshoe option	An option given to an underwriter of common stock that will allow it to purchase up to an additional 15% of the offering from the issuer at the original offering price to cover over-allotments for securities that are in high demand.
gross domestic product (GDP)	The value of all goods and services produced by a country within a period of time. GDP includes government purchases, investments, and exports minus imports.
gross income	All income received by a taxpayer before deductions for taxes.
gross revenue pledge	A flow-of-funds pledge for a municipal revenue bond that states that debt service will be paid first.

growth fund	A fund whose objective is capital appreciation. Growth funds invest in common stocks to achieve their objective.
growth stock	The stock of a company whose earnings grow at a rate that is faster than the growth rate of the economy as a whole. Growth stocks are characterized by increased opportunities for appreciation and little or no dividends.
guardian	An individual who has a fiduciary responsibility for another, usually a minor.

H

halt	A temporary stop in the trading of a security. If a common stock is halted, all derivatives and convertibles will be halted as well.
head and shoulders	A chart pattern that indicates a reversal of a trend. A head-and-shoulders top indicates a reversal of an uptrend and is considered bearish. A head-and-shoulders bottom is the reversal of a downtrend and is considered bullish.
hedge	A position taken in a security to offset or reduce the risk associated with the risk of another security.
HH bond	A nonmarketable government security that pays semiannual interest. Series HH bonds are issued with a $500 minimum value and may only be purchased by trading matured Series EE bonds; they may not be purchased with cash.
high	The highest price paid for a security during a trading session or during a 52-week period.
holder	An individual or corporation that owns a security. The holder of a security is also known as being long the security.
holding period	The length of time during which an investor owns a security. The holding period is important for calculating tax liability.
hold in street name	The registration of customer securities in the name of the broker dealer. Most customers register securities in the name of the broker dealer to make the transfer of ownership easier.
horizontal spread	Also known as a calendar spread. The simultaneous purchase and sale of two calls or two puts on the same underlying security with the same exercise price but with different expiration months.
hot issue	A new issue of securities that trades at an immediate premium to its offering price in the secondary market.
HR 10 plan	See Keogh plan.
hypothecation	The customer's pledge of securities as collateral for a margin loan.

I

immediate annuity	An annuity contract purchased with a single payment that entitles the holder to receive immediate payments from the contract. The annuitant purchases annuity units and usually begins receiving payments within 60 days.
immediate family	An individual's immediate family includes parents, parents-in-law, children, spouse, and any relative financially dependent upon the individual.
immediate or cancel (IOC)	An order that is to be executed as fully as possible immediately and whatever is not executed will be canceled.
income bond	A highly speculative bond that is issued at a discount from par and only pays interest if the issuer has enough income to do so. The issuer of the income bond only promises to pay principal at maturity. Income bonds trade flat without accrued interest.
income fund	A mutual fund whose investment objective is to achieve current income for its shareholders by investing in bonds and preferred stocks.
income program	A type of oil and gas program that purchases producing wells to receive the income received from the sale of the proven reserves.
income statement	A financial statement that shows a corporation's revenue and expenses for the time period in question.
indefeasible title	A record of ownership that cannot be challenged.
index	A representation of the price action of a given group of securities. Indexes are used to measure the condition of the market as a whole, such as with the S&P 500, or can be used to measure the condition of an industry group, such as with the Biotech index.
index option	An option on an underlying financial index. Index options settle in cash.
indication of interest	An investor's expression of a willingness to purchase a new issue of securities after receiving a preliminary prospectus. The investor's indication of interest is not binding on either the investor or the firm.
Individual Retirement Account (IRA)	A self-directed retirement account that allows individuals with earned income to contribute the lesser of 100% of earned income or the annual maximum per year. The contributions may be made with pre- or after-tax dollars, depending on the individual's level of income and whether he or she is eligible to participate in an employer's sponsored plan.
industrial development bond	A private-purpose municipal bond whose proceeds are used to build a facility that is leased to a corporation. The debt service on the bonds is supported by the lease payments.
inflation	The persistent upward pressure on the price of goods and services over time.
initial margin requirement	The initial amount of equity that a customer must deposit to establish a position. The initial margin requirement is set by the Federal Reserve Board under Regulation T.
initial public offering (IPO)	The first offering of common stock to the general investing public.
in part call	A partial call of a bond issue for redemption.

inside information	Information that is not known to people outside of the corporation. Information becomes public only after it is released by the corporation through a recognized media source. Inside information may be both material and immaterial. It is only illegal to trade on inside material information.
inside market	The highest bid and the lowest offer for a security.
insider	A company's officers, directors, large stockholders of 10% or more of the company, and anyone who is in possession of nonpublic material information, along with the immediate family members of the same.
Insider Trading and Securities Fraud Enforcement Act of 1988	Federal legislation that made the penalties for people trading on material nonpublic information more severe. Penalties for insider traders are up to the greater of 300% of the amount of money made or the loss avoided or $1 million and up to 5 years in prison. People who disseminate inside information may be imprisoned and fined up to $1 million.
INSTINET	A computer network that facilitates trading of large blocks of stocks between institutions without the use of a broker dealer.
institutional account	An account in the name of an institution but operated for the benefit of others (i.e., banks and mutual funds). There is no minimum size for an institutional account.
institutional communication	Any communication that is distributed exclusively to institutional investors. Institutional communication does not require the preapproval of a principal but must be maintained for 3 years by the firm.
institutional investor	An investor who trades for its own account or for the accounts of others in large quantities and is covered by fewer protective laws.
insurance covenant	The promise of an issuer of revenue bonds to maintain insurance on the financed project.
intangible asset	Nonphysical property of a corporation, such as trademarks and copyrights.
intangible drilling cost (IDC)	Costs for an oil and gas program that are expensed in the year in which they are incurred for such things as wages, surveys, and well casings.
interbank market	An international currency market.
interest	The cost for borrowing money, usually charged at an annual percentage rate.
interest rate option	An option based on U.S. government securities. The options are either rate-based or priced-based options.
interest rate risk	The risk borne by investors in interest-bearing securities, which subjects the holder to a loss of principal should interest rates rise.
interlocking directorate	Corporate boards that share one or more directors.
Internal Revenue Code (IRC)	The codes that define tax liabilities for U.S. taxpayers.
interpositioning	The placing of another broker dealer in between the customer and the best market. Interpositioning is prohibited unless it can be demonstrated that the customer received a better price because of it.

interstate offering	A multistate offering of securities that requires that the issuer register with the SEC as well as with the states in which the securities will be sold.
in the money	A relationship between the strike price of an option and the underlying security's price. A call is in the money when the strike price is lower than the security's price. A put is in the money when the strike price is higher than the security's price.
intrastate offering	*See* Rule 147.
intrinsic value	The amount by which an option is in the money.
introducing broker	*See* correspondent broker dealer.
inverted yield curve	A yield curve where the cost of short-term financing exceeds the cost of long-term financing.
investment adviser	Anyone who charges a fee for investment advice or who holds himself out to the public as being in the business of giving investment advice for a fee.
Investment Advisers Act of 1940	The federal legislation that sets forth guidelines for business requirements and activities of investment advisers.
investment banker	A financial institution that is in the business of raising capital for companies and municipalities by underwriting securities.
investment company	A company that sells undivided interests in a pool of securities and manages the portfolio for the benefit of the investors. Investment companies include management companies, unit investment trusts, and face-amount companies.
Investment Company Act of 1940	Federal legislation that regulates the operation and registration of investment companies.
investment-grade security	A security that has been assigned a rating in the highest rating tier by a recognized ratings agency.
investment objective	An investor's set of goals as to how he or she is seeking to make money, such as capital appreciation or current income.
investor	The purchaser of a security who seeks to realize a profit.
IRA rollover	The temporary distribution of assets from an IRA and the subsequent reinvestment of the assets into another IRA within 60 days. An IRA may be rolled over only once per year and is subject to a 10% penalty and ordinary income taxes if the investor is under 59-1/2 and if the assets are not deposited in another qualified account within 60 days.
IRA transfer	The movement of assets from one qualified account to another without the account holder taking possession of the assets. Investors may transfer an IRA as often as they like.
issued stock	Stock that has actually been sold to the investing public.
issuer	Any entity that issues or proposes to issue securities.

J

joint account	An account that is owned by two or more parties. Joint accounts allow either party to enter transactions for the account. Both parties must sign a joint account agreement. All joint accounts must be designated as joint tenants in common or with rights of survivorship.
joint tenants in common (JTIC)	A joint account where the assets of a party who has died transfer to the decedent's estate, not the other tenant.
joint tenants with rights of survivorship (JTWROS)	A joint account where the assets of a party who has died transfer to the surviving party, not the decedent's estate.
joint venture	An interest in an operation shared by two or more parties. The parties have no other relationship beyond the joint venture.
junk bond	A bond with a high degree of default risk that has been assigned a speculative rating by the ratings agencies.
junk bond fund	A speculative bond fund that invests in high-yield bonds in order to achieve a high degree of current income.

K

Keogh plan	A qualified retirement account for self-employed individuals. Contributions are limited to the lesser of 20% of their gross income or up to the annual limit.
Keynesian economics	An economic theory that states that government intervention in the marketplace helps sustain economic growth.
know-your-customer rule	Industry regulation that requires a registered representative to be familiar with the customer's financial objectives and needs prior to making a recommendation; also known as Rule 405.

L

lagging indicator	A measurement of economic activity that changes after a change has taken place in economic activity. Lagging indicators are useful confirmation tools when determining the strength of an economic trend. Lagging indicators include corporate profits, average duration of unemployment, and labor costs.
last in, first out (LIFO)	An accounting method used that states that the last item that was produced is the first item sold.
leading indicator	A measurement of economic activity that changes prior to a change in economic activity. Leading economic indicators are useful in predicting a coming trend in economic activity. Leading economic indicators include housing permits, new orders for durable goods, and the S&P 500.

LEAPS (long-term equity anticipation securities)	A long-term option on a security that has an expiration of up to 39 months.
lease rental bonds	A municipal bond that is issued to finance the building of a facility that will be rented out. The lease payments on the facility will support the bond's debt service.
legal list	A list of securities that have been approved by certain state securities regulators for purchase by fiduciaries.
legal opinion	An opinion issued by a bond attorney stating that the issue is a legally binding obligation of the state or municipality. The legal opinion also contains a statement regarding the tax status of the interest payments received by investors.
legislative risk	The risk that the government may do something that adversely affects an investment.
letter of intent (LOI)	A letter signed by the purchaser of mutual fund shares that states the investor's intention to invest a certain amount of money over a 13-month period. By agreeing to invest this sum, the investor is entitled to receive a lower sales charge on all purchases covered by the letter of intent. The letter of intent may be backdated up to 90 days from an initial purchase. Should the investor fail to invest the stated sum, a sales charge adjustment will be charged.
level load	A mutual fund share that charges a flat annual fee, such as a 12B-1 fee.
level one	A Nasdaq workstation service that allows the agent to see the inside market only.
level two	A Nasdaq workstation service that allows the order-entry firm to see the inside market, to view the quotes entered by all market makers, and to execute orders.
level three	A Nasdaq workstation service that allows market-making firms to see the inside market, to view the quotes entered by all market makers, to execute orders, and to enter their own quotes for the security. This is the highest level of Nasdaq service.
leverage	The use of borrowed funds to try to obtain a rate of return that exceeds the cost of the funds.
liability	A legal obligation to pay a debt either incurred through borrowing or through the normal course of business.
life annuity/straight life	An annuity payout option that provides payments over the life of the annuitant.
life annuity with period certain	An annuity payout option that provides payments to the annuitant for life or to the annuitant's estate for the period certain, whichever is longer.
life contingency	An annuity payout option that provides a death benefit in case the annuitant dies during the accumulation stage.
limit order	An order that sets a maximum price that the investor will pay in the case of a buy order or the minimum price the investor will accept in the case of a sell order.
limited liability	A protection afforded to investors in securities that limits their liability to the amount of money invested in the securities.
limited partner	A passive investor in a direct participation program who has no role in the project's management.

limited partnership (LP)	An association of two or more partners with at least one partner being the general partner who is responsible for the management of the partnership.
limited partnership agreement	The foundation of all limited partnerships. The agreement is the contract between all partners, and it spells out the authority of the general partner and the rights of all limited partners.
limited power of attorney/limited trading authorization	Legal authorization for a representative or a firm to affect purchases and sales for a customer's account without the customer's prior knowledge. The authorization is limited to buying and selling securities and may not be given to another party.
limited principal	An individual who has passed the Series 26 exam and may supervise Series 6 limited representatives.
limited representative	An individual who has passed the Series 6 exam and may represent a broker dealer in the sale of mutual fund shares and variable contracts.
limited tax bond	A type of general obligation bond that is issued by a municipality that may not increase its tax rate to pay the debt service of the issue.
liquidity	The ability of an investment to be readily converted into cash.
liquidity risk	The risk that an investor may not be able to sell a security when needed or that selling a security when needed will adversely affect the price.
listed option	A standardized option contract that is traded on an exchange.
listed security	A security that trades on one of the exchanges. Only securities that trade on an exchange are known as listed securities.
loan consent agreement	A portion of the margin agreement that allows the broker dealer to loan out the customer's securities to another customer who wishes to borrow them to sell the security short.
locked market	A market condition that results when the bid and the offer for a security are equal.
LOI	*See* letter of intent.
London Interbank Offered Rate (LIBOR)	The interbank rates for dollar-denominated deposits in England.
long	A term used to describe an investor who owns a security.
long market value	The total long market value of a customer's account.
long-term gain	A profit realized through the sale of a security at a price that is higher than its purchase price after being held for more than 12 months.
long-term loss	A loss realized through the sale of a security at a price that is lower than its purchase price after being held for more than 12 months.
loss carry forward	A capital loss realized on the sale of an asset in 1 year that is carried forward in whole or part to subsequent tax years.
low	The lowest price at which a security has traded in any given period, usually measured during a trading day or for 52 weeks.

M

M1	The most liquid measure of the money supply. It includes all currency and demand and NOW deposits (checking accounts).
M2	A measure of the money supply that includes M1 plus all time deposits, savings accounts, and noninstitutional money market accounts.
M3	A measure of the money supply that includes M2 and large time deposits, institutional money market funds, short-term repurchase agreements, and other large liquid assets.
maintenance call	A demand for additional cash or collateral made by a broker dealer when a margin customer's account equity has fallen below the minimum requirement of the NYSE or that is set by the broker dealer.
maintenance covenant	A promise made by an issuer of a municipal revenue bond to maintain the facility in good repair.
Major Market Index (XMI)	An index created by the Amex to AMEX 15 of the 30 largest stocks in the Dow Jones Industrial Average.
Maloney Act of 1938	An amendment to the Securities Exchange Act of 1934 that gave the NASD (now part of FINRA) the authority to regulate the over-the-counter market.
managed underwriting	An underwriting conducted by a syndicate led by the managing underwriter.
management company	A type of investment company that actively manages a portfolio of securities in order to meet a stated investment objective. Management companies are also known as mutual funds.
management fee	(1) The fee received by the lead or managing underwriter of a syndicate. (2) The fee received by a sponsor of a direct participation program.
managing partner	The general partner in a direct participation program.
managing underwriter	The lead underwriter in a syndicate who is responsible for negotiating with the issuer, forming the syndicate, and settling the syndicate account.
margin	The amount of customer equity that is required to hold a position in a security.
margin account	An account that allows the customer to borrow money from the brokerage firm to buy securities.
margin call	A demand for cash or collateral mandated by the Federal Reserve Board under Regulation T.
margin department	The department in a broker dealer that calculates money owed by the customer or money due the customer.
margin maintenance call	*See* maintenance call.
mark to the market	The monitoring of the current value of a position relative to the price at which the trade was executed for securities purchased on margin or on a when-issued basis.
markdown	The profit earned by a dealer on a transaction when purchasing securities for its own account from a customer.

marketability	The ability of an investment to be exchanged between two investors. A security with an active secondary market has a higher level of marketability than one whose market is not as active.
market arbitrage	A type of arbitrage that consists of purchasing a security in one marketplace and selling it in another to take advantage of price inefficiencies.
market letter	A regular publication, usually issued by an investment adviser, that offers information and/or advice regarding securities, market conditions, or the economy as a whole.
market maker	A Nasdaq firm that is required to quote a continuous two-sided market for the securities in which it trades.
market not held	A type of order that gives the floor broker discretion over the time and price of execution.
market on close	An order that will be executed at whatever price the market is at, either on the closing print or just prior to the closing print.
market on open	An order that will be executed at whatever price the market is at, either on the opening print or just after the opening print.
market order	A type of order that will be executed immediately at the best available price once it is presented to the market.
market-out clause	A clause in an underwriting agreement that gives the syndicate the ability to cancel the underwriting if it finds a material problem with the information or condition of the issuer.
market risk/ systematic risk	The risk inherent in any investment in the market that states an investor may lose money simply because the market is going down.
market value	The value of a security that is determined in the marketplace by the investors who enter bids and offers for a security.
markup	The compensation paid to a securities dealer for selling a security to a customer from its inventory.
markup policy	FINRA's guideline that states that the price that is paid or received by an investor must be reasonably related to the market price for that security. FINRA offers 5% as a guideline for what is reasonable to charge investors when they purchase or sell securities.
material information	Information that would affect a company's current or future prospects or an investor's decision to invest in the company.
maturity date	The date on which a bond's principal amount becomes payable to its holders.
member	A member of FINRA or one of the 1,366 members of the NYSE.
member firm	A firm that is a member of the NYSE, FINRA, or another self-regulatory organization.
member order	A retail order entered by a member of a municipal bond syndicate for which the member will receive all of the sales credit.
mini maxi underwriting	A type of best efforts underwriting that states that the offering will not become effective until a minimum amount is sold and sets a maximum amount that may be sold.

minimum death benefit	The minimum guaranteed death benefit that will be paid to the beneficiaries if the holder of a variable life insurance policy dies.
minus tick	A trade in an exchange-listed security that is at a price that is lower than the previous trade.
modern portfolio theory	An investing approach that looks at the overall return and risk of a portfolio as a whole, not as a collection of single investments.
modified accelerated cost recovery system (MACRS)	An accounting method that allows the owner to recover a larger portion of the asset's value in the early years of its life.
monetarist theory	A theory that states that the money supply is the driving force in the economy and that a well-managed money supply will benefit the economy.
monetary policy	Economic policy that is controlled by the Federal Reserve Board and controls the amount of money in circulation and the level of interest rates.
money market	The secondary market where short-term highly liquid securities are traded. Securities traded in the money market include T-bills, negotiable CDs, bankers' acceptances, commercial paper, and other short-term securities with less than 12 months to maturity.
money market mutual fund	A mutual fund that invests in money market instruments to generate monthly interest for its shareholders. Money market mutual funds have a stable NAV that is equal to $1, but it is not guaranteed.
money supply	The total amount of currency, loans, and credit in the economy. The money supply is measured by M1, M2, M3, and L.
moral obligation bond	A type of municipal revenue bond that will allow the state or municipality to vote to cover a shortfall in the debt service.
multiplier effect	The ability of the money supply to grow simply through the normal course of banking. When banks and other financial institutions accept deposits and subsequently loan out those deposits to earn interest, the amount of money in the system grows.
municipal bond	A bond issued by a state or political subdivision of a state in an effort to finance its operations. Interest earned by investors in municipal bonds is almost always free from federal income taxes.
municipal bond fund	A mutual fund that invests in a portfolio of municipal debt in an effort to produce income that is free from federal income taxes for its investors.
Municipal Bond Investors Assurance Corp. (MBIA)	An independent insurance company that will, for a fee received from the issuer, insure the interest and principal payments on a municipal bond.
municipal note	A short-term municipal issue sold to manage the issuer's cash flow, usually in anticipation of the offering of long-term financing.
Municipal Securities Rulemaking Board (MSRB)	The self-regulatory organization that oversees the issuance and trading of municipal bonds. The MSRB's rules are enforced by other industry SROs.

Munifacts	A service that provides real-time secondary market quotes. Munifacts is now known as Thomson Muni Market Monitor.
mutual fund	An investment company that invests in and manages a portfolio of securities for its shareholders. Open-end mutual funds sell their shares to investors on a continuous basis and must stand ready to redeem their shares upon the shareholder's request.
mutual fund custodian	A qualified financial institution that maintains physical custody of a mutual fund's cash and securities. Custodians are usually banks, trust companies, or exchange member firms.

N

naked	The sale of a call option without owning the underlying security or the sale of a put option without being short the stock or having cash on deposit that is sufficient to purchase the underlying security.
narrow-based index	An index that is based on a market sector or a limited number of securities.
National Securities Clearing Corporation (NSCC)	The clearing intermediary through which clearing member firms reconcile their securities accounts.
NAV (net asset value)	The net value of a mutual fund after deducting all its liabilities. A mutual fund must calculate its NAV at least once per business day. To determine NAV per share, simply divide the mutual fund's NAV by the total number of shares outstanding.
negotiability	The ability of an investment to be freely exchanged between noninterested parties.
negotiable certificate of deposit	A certificate issued by a bank for a time deposit in excess of $100,000 that can be exchanged between parties prior to its maturity date. FDIC insurance only covers the first $250,000 of the principal amount should the bank fail.
NOW (negotiable order of withdrawal) Account	A type of demand deposit that allows the holder to write checks against an interest-bearing account.
net change	The difference between the previous day's closing price and the price of the most recently reported trade for a security.
net current assets per share	A calculation of the value per share that excludes fixed assets and intangibles.
net debt per capita	A measure of a municipal issuer's ability to meet its obligations. It measures the debt level of the issuer in relation to the population.
net debt to assessed valuation	A measure of the issuer's ability to meet its obligations and to raise additional revenue through property taxes.
net direct debt	The total amount of general obligation debt, including notes and short-term financing, issued by a municipality or state.

net interest cost (NIC)	A calculation that measures the interest cost of a municipal issue over the life of all bonds. Most competitive underwritings for municipal securities are awarded to the syndicate that submits the bid with the lowest NIC.
net investment income	The total sum of investment income derived from dividend and interest income after subtracting expenses.
net revenue pledge	A pledge from a revenue bond that pays maintenance and operation expenses first, then debt service.
net total debt	The total of a municipality's direct debt plus its overlapping debt.
net worth	The value of a corporation after subtracting all of its liabilities. A corporation's net worth is also equal to shareholder's equity.
new account form	Paperwork that must be filled out and signed by the representative and a principal of the firm prior to the opening of any account being opened for a customer.
new construction program	A real estate program that seeks to achieve capital appreciation by building new properties.
new housing authority (NHA)	A municipal bond issued to build low-income housing. NHA bonds are guaranteed by the U.S. government and are considered the safest type of municipal bonds. NHA bonds are not considered to be double-barreled bonds.
new issue	*See* initial public offering (IPO).
New York Stock Exchange (NYSE)	A membership organization that provides a marketplace for securities to be exchanged in one centralized location through a dual-auction process.
no-load fund	A fund that does not charge the investor a sales charge to invest in the fund. Shares of no-load mutual funds are sold directly from the fund company to the investor.
nominal owner	An individual or entity registered as the owner of record of securities for the benefit of another party.
nominal quote	A quote given for informational purposes only. A trader who identifies a quote as being nominal cannot be held to trading at the prices that were clearly identified as being nominal.
nominal yield	The yield that is stated or named on the security. The nominal yield, once it has been set, never changes, regardless of the market price of the security.
noncompetitive bid	A bid submitted for Treasury bills where the purchaser agrees to accept the average of all yields accepted at the auction. Noncompetitive tenders are always the first orders filled at the auction.
noncumulative preferred	A type of preferred stock whose dividends do not accumulate in arrears if the issuer misses the payment.
nondiscrimination	A clause that states that all eligible individuals must be allowed to participate in a qualified retirement plan.
nondiversification	An investment strategy that concentrates its investments among a small group of securities or issuers.
nondiversified management company	An investment company that concentrates its investments among a few issuers or securities and does not meet the diversification requirements of the Investment Company Act of 1940.

nonfixed UIT	A type of UIT that allows changes in the portfolio and traditionally invests in mutual fund shares.
nonqualified retirement plan	A retirement plan that does not allow contributions to be made with pre-tax dollars; that is, the retirement plan does not qualify for beneficial tax treatment from the IRS for its contributions.
nonsystematic risk	A risk that is specific to an issuer or an industry.
note	An intermediate-term interest-bearing security that represents an obligation of its issuer.
not-held (NH) order	An order that gives the floor broker discretion as to the time and price of execution.
numbered account	An account that has been designated a number for identification purposes in order to maintain anonymity for its owner. The owner must sign a statement acknowledging ownership.

O

odd lot	A transaction that is for less than 100 shares of stock or for less than 5 bonds.
odd lot differential	An additional fee that may be charged to an investor for the handling of odd lot transactions (usually waived).
odd lot theory	A contrarian theory that states that small investors will invariably buy and sell at the wrong time.
offer	A price published at which an investor or broker dealer is willing to sell a security.
offering circular	The offering document that is prepared by a corporation selling securities under a Regulation A offering.
office of supervisory jurisdiction (OSJ)	An office identified by the broker dealer as having supervisory responsibilities for agents. It has final approval of new accounts, makes markets, and structures offerings.
Office of the Comptroller of the Currency	An office of the U.S. Treasury that is responsible for regulating the practices of national banks.
official notice of sale	The notice of sale published in the *Daily Bond Buyer* by a municipal issuer that is used to obtain an underwriter for municipal bonds.
official statement	The offering document for a municipal issuer that must be provided to every purchaser if the issuer prepares one.
oil and gas direct participation program	A type of direct participation program designed to invest in oil and gas production or exploration.
oil depletion allowance	An accounting method used to reduce the amount of reserves available from a producing well.
omnibus account	An account used by an introducing member to execute and clear all of its customers' trades.
open-end covenant	A type of bond indenture that allows for the issuance of additional bonds with the same claim on the collateral as the original issue.

open-end investment company	*See* mutual fund.
option	A contract between two investors to purchase or sell a security at a given price for a certain period of time.
option agreement	A form that must be signed and returned by an option investor within 15 days of the account's approval to trade options.
option disclosure document	A document that must be furnished to all option investors at the time the account is approved for options trading. It is published by the Options Clearing Corporation (OCC), and it details the risks and features of standardized options.
Options Clearing Corporation (OCC)	The organization that issues and guarantees the performance of standardized options.
order book official (OBO)	Employees of the CBOE who are responsible for maintaining a fair and orderly market in the options assigned to them and for executing orders that have been left with them.
order department	The department of a broker dealer that is responsible for routing orders to the markets for execution.
order memorandum/ order ticket	The written document filled out by a registered representative that identifies, among other things, the security, the amount, the customer, and the account number for which the order is being entered.
original issue discount (OID)	A bond that has been issued to the public at a discount to its par value. The OID on a corporate bond is taxed as if it was earned annually. The OID on a municipal bond is exempt from taxation.
OTC market	*See* over-the-counter (OTC) market.
out of the money	The relationship of an option's strike price to the underlying security's price when exercising the option would not make economic sense. A call is out of the money when the security's price is below the option's strike price. A put is out of the money when the security's price is above the option's strike price.
outstanding stock	The total amount of a security that has been sold to the investing public and that remains in the hands of the investing public.
overlapping debt	The portion of another taxing authority's debt that a municipality is responsible for.
overriding royalty interest	A type of sharing arrangement that offers an individual with no risk a portion of the revenue in exchange for something of value, such as the right to drill on the owner's land.
over-the-counter (OTC) market	An interdealer market that consists of a computer and phone network through which broker dealers trade securities.

P

par	The stated principal amount of a security. Par value is of great importance for fixed-income securities such as bonds or preferred stock. Par value for bonds is traditionally $1,000, whereas par for a preferred stock is normally $100. Par value is of little importance when looking at common stock.
parity	A condition that results when the value of an underlying common stock to be received upon conversion equals the value of the convertible security.
partial call	A call of a portion of an issuer's callable securities.
participation	The code set forth in the Employee Retirement Income Security Act of 1974 that states who is eligible to participate in an employer sponsored retirement plan.
passive income	Income received by an individual for which no work was performed, such as rental income received from a rental property.
passive loss	A loss realized on an investment in a limited partnership or rental property that can be used to offset passive income.
pass-through certificate	A security that passes through income and principal payments made to an underlying portfolio of mortgages. Ginnie Mae is one of the biggest issuers of this type of security.
payment date	The day when a dividend will actually be sent to investors. The payment date is set by the corporation's board of directors at the time when they initially declare the dividend.
payout stage	The period during which an annuitant receives payments from an annuity contract.
payroll deduction plan	A nonqualified retirement plan where employees authorize the employer to take regular deductions from their paychecks to invest in a retirement account.
pension plan	A contractual retirement plan between an employee and an employer that is designed to provide regular income for the employee after retirement.
percentage depletion	An accounting method that allows for a tax deduction for the reduction of reserves.
periodic payment plan	A contract to purchase mutual fund shares over an extended period of time, usually in exchange for the fund company waiving its minimum investment requirement.
person	Any individual or entity that can enter into a legally binding contract for the purchase and sale of securities.
personal income	Income earned by an individual from providing services and through investments.
phantom income	(1) A term used to describe the taxable appreciation on a zero-coupon bond. (2) The term used to describe taxable income generated by a limited partnership that is not producing positive cash flow.
PINK OTC	An electronic quote service containing quotes for unlisted securities that is published by the OTC Markets Group.
placement ratio	A ratio that details the percentage of municipal bonds sold, relative to the number of bonds offered in the last week, published by the *Daily Bond Buyer*.
plus tick	A transaction in an exchange-listed security that is higher than the previous transaction.

point	An increment of change in the price of a security: 1 bond point equals 1% of par or 1% of $1,000, or $10.
POP	See public offering price (POP).
portfolio income	Interest and dividends earned through investing in securities.
portfolio manager	An entity that is hired to manage the investment portfolios of a mutual fund. The portfolio manager is paid a fee that is based on the net assets of the fund.
position	The amount of a security in which an investor has an interest by either being long (owning) or short (owing) the security.
power of substitution	See stock power.
preemptive right	The right of a common stockholder to maintain proportional ownership interest in a security. A corporation may not issue additional shares of common stock without first offering those shares to existing stockholders.
preferred stock	An equity security issued with a stated dividend rate. Preferred stockholders have a higher claim on a corporation's dividends and assets than common holders.
preferred stock ratio	A ratio detailing the amount of an issuer's total capitalization that is made up of preferred stock. The ratio is found by dividing the total par value of preferred stock by the issuer's total capitalization.
preliminary prospectus/red herring	A document used to solicit indications of interest during the cooling-off period for a new issue of securities. All of the information in the preliminary prospectus is subject to revision and change. The cover of a preliminary prospectus must have a statement saying that the securities have not yet become registered and that they may not be sold until the registration becomes effective. This statement is written in red ink, and this is where the term *red herring* comes from.
price-earnings ratio (PE)	A measure of value used by analysts. It is calculated by dividing the issuer's stock price by its earnings per share.
price spread	A term used to describe an option spread where the long and short options differ only in their exercise prices.
primary earnings per share	The amount of earnings available per common share prior to the conversion of any outstanding convertible securities.
prime rate	The interest rate that banks charge their best corporate customers on loans.
principal	(1) The face amount of a bond. (2) A broker dealer trading for its own account. (3) An individual who has successfully completed a principal exam and may supervise representatives.
principal transaction	A transaction where a broker dealer participates in a trade by buying or selling securities for its own account.
priority	The acceptance of bids and offers for exchange-listed securities on a first-come, first-served (FCFS) basis.
private placement	The private sale of securities to a limited number of investors. Also known as a Regulation D offering.
profit sharing plan	A plan that allows the employer to distribute a percentage of its profits to its employees at a predetermined rate. The money may be paid directly to the employee or deposited into a retirement account.

progressive tax	A tax structure where the tax rate increases as the income level of the individual or entity increases.
project note	A municipal bond issued as interim financing in anticipation of the issuance of new housing authority bonds.
prospectus	See final prospectus.
proxy	A limited authority given by stockholders to another party to vote their shares in a corporate election. The stockholder may specify how the votes are cast or may give the party discretion.
proxy department	The department in a brokerage firm that is responsible for forwarding proxies and financial information to investors whose stock is held in street name.
prudent man rule	A rule that governs investments made by fiduciaries for the benefit of a third party. The rule states that the investments must be similar to those that a prudent person would make for him- or herself.
public offering	The sale of securities by an issuer to public investors.
public offering price (POP)	The price paid by an investor to purchase open-end mutual fund shares. Also the price set for a security the first time it is sold to the investing public.
put	An option contract that allows the buyer to sell a security at a set price for a specific period of time. The seller of a put is obligated to purchase the security at a set price for a specific period of time, should the buyer exercise the option.
put buyer	A bearish investor who pays a premium for the right to sell a security at a set price for a certain period of time.
put spread	An option position created by the simultaneous purchase and sale of two put options on the same underlying security that differ in strike prices, expiration months, or both.
put writer	A bullish investor who sells a put option in order to receive the option premium. The writer is obligated to purchase the security if the buyer exercises the option.

Q

qualified legal opinion	A legal opinion containing conditions or reservations relating to the issue. A legal opinion is issued by a bond counsel for a municipal issuer.
qualified retirement plan	A retirement plan that qualifies for favorable tax treatment by the IRS for contributions made into the plan.
quick assets	A measure of liquidity that subtracts the value of a corporation's unsold inventory from its current assets.
quick ratio	See acid-test ratio.
quote	A bid and offer broadcast from the exchange or through the Nasdaq system that displays the prices at which a security may be purchased and sold and in what quantities.

R

range	The price difference between the high and low for a security.
rate covenant	A promise in the trust indenture of a municipal revenue bond to keep the user fees high enough to support the debt service.
rating	A judgment of an issuer's ability to meet its credit obligations. The higher the credit quality of the issuer is, the higher the credit rating. The lower the credit quality is, the lower the credit rating, and the higher the risk associated with the securities.
rating service	Major financial organizations that evaluate the credit quality of issuers. Issuers have to request and pay for the service. Standard and Poor's, Moody's, and Fitch are the most widely followed rating services.
raw land program	A type of real estate limited partnership that invests in land for capital appreciation.
real estate investment trust (REIT)	An entity that is organized to invest in or manage real estate. REITs offer investors certain tax advantages and can avoid double taxation if the REIT passes through at least 90 % of net investment income.
real estate limited partnership	A type of direct participation program that invests in real estate projects to produce income or capital appreciation.
real estate mortgage investment conduit (REMIC)	An organization that pools investors' capital to purchase portfolios of mortgages.
realized gain	A profit earned on the sale of a security at a price that exceeds its purchase price.
realized loss	A loss recognized by an investor by selling a security at a price that is less than its purchase price.
reallowance	A sales concession available to dealers who sell securities subject to an offering who are not syndicate or selling group members.
recapture	An event that causes a tax liability on a previously taken deduction, such as selling an asset above its depreciated cost base.
recession	A decline in GDP that lasts for at least 6 months but not longer than 18 months.
reclamation	The right of a seller to demand or claim any loss from the buying party due to the buyer's failure to settle the transaction.
record date	A date set by a corporation's board of directors that determines which shareholders will be entitled to receive a declared dividend. Shareholders must be owners of record on this date in order to collect the dividend.
recourse loan	A loan taken out by a limited partnership that allows the lender to seek payment from the limited partners in the case of the partnership's failure to pay.
redeemable security	A security that can be redeemed by the issuer at the investor's request. Open-end mutual funds are an example of redeemable securities.
redemption	The return of an investor's capital by an issuer. Open-end mutual funds must redeem their securities within 7 days of an investor's request.
red herring	*See* preliminary prospectus.
registered	A term that describes the level of owner information that is recorded by the security's issuer.

registered as to principal only	A type of bond registration that requires the investor to clip coupons to receive the bond's interest payments. The issuer will automatically send the investor the bond's principal amount at maturity.
registered options principal (ROP)	An individual who has passed the Series 4 exam.
registered principal	A supervisor of a member firm who has passed the principal examination.
registered representative	An individual who has successfully completed a qualified examination to represent a broker dealer or issuer in securities transactions.
registrar	An independent organization that accounts for all outstanding stock and bonds of an issuer.
registration statement	The full disclosure statement that nonexempt issuers must file with the SEC prior to offering securities for sale to the public. The Securities Act of 1933 requires that a registration statement be filed.
regressive tax	A tax that is levied on all parties at the same rate, regardless of their income. An example of a regressive tax is a sales tax. A larger percentage of a low-income earner's income is taken away by the tax.
regular-way settlement	The standard number of business days in which a securities transaction is completed and paid for. Corporate securities and municipal bonds settle the regular way on the second business day after the trade date with payment due on the fourth business day. Government securities settle the next business day.
regulated investment company	An investment company that qualifies as a conduit for net investment income under Internal Revenue Code subchapter M, so long as it distributes at least 90% of its net investment income to shareholders.
Regulation A	A Regulation A offering allows a company to raise up to 75 million dollars in a tier 2 offering and up to 20 million dollars in a tier 1 offering in any 12-month period.
Regulation D	A private placement or sale of securities that allows for an exemption from registration under the Securities Act of 1933. A private placement may be sold to an unlimited number of accredited investors but may only be sold to 35 nonaccredited investors in any 12-month period.
Regulation G	Regulates the extension of credit for securities purchases by other commercial lenders.
Regulation T	Regulates the extension of credit by broker dealers for securities purchases.
Regulation U	Regulates the extension of credit by banks for securities purchases.
Regulation X	Regulates the extension of credit by overseas lenders for securities purchases.
Rehypothecation	The act of a broker dealer repledging a customer's securities as collateral at a bank to obtain a loan for the customer.
REIT	See real estate investment trust (REIT).
rejection	The act of a buyer of a security refusing delivery.
reorganization department	The department in a brokerage firm that handles changes in securities that result from a merger or acquisition or calls.
repurchase agreement (REPO)	A fully collateralized loan that results in a sale of securities to the lender, with the borrower agreeing to repurchase them at a higher price in the future. The higher price represents the lender's interest.

reserve maintenance fund	An account set up to provide additional funds to maintain a revenue-producing facility financed by a revenue bond.
reserve requirement	A deposit required to be placed on account with the Federal Reserve Board by banks. The requirement is a percentage of the bank's customers' deposits.
resistance	A price level to which a security appreciates and attracts sellers. The new sellers keep the security's price from rising any higher.
restricted account	(1) A long margin account that has less than 50% equity but more than 25% or a short margin account that has equity of less than 50% but more than 30%. (2) A customer account that has been subject to a sellout.
restricted stock	A nonexempt unregistered security that has been obtained by means other than a public offering.
retail communication	Any communication that may be seen in whole or in part by an individual investor. Retail communication must be approved by a principal prior to first use and maintained by the firm for 3 years.
retained earnings	The amount of a corporation's net income that has not been paid out to shareholders as dividends.
retention	The amount of a new issue that an underwriter allocates to its own clients.
retention requirement	The amount of equity that must be left in a restricted margin account when withdrawing securities.
return on equity	A measure of performance found by dividing after-tax income by common stockholders' equity.
return on investment (ROI)	The profit or loss realized by an investor from holding a security expressed as a percentage of the invested capital.
revenue anticipation note	A short-term municipal issue that is sold to manage an issuer's cash flow in anticipation of other revenue in the future.
reverse repurchase agreement	A fully collateralized loan that results in the purchase of securities with the intention of reselling them to the borrower at a higher price. The higher price represents the buyer's/lender's interest.
reverse split	A stock split that results in fewer shares outstanding, with each share being worth proportionally more.
reversionary working interest	A revenue-sharing arrangement where the general partner shares none of the cost and receives none of the revenue until the limited partners have received their payments back, plus any predetermined amount of return.
right	A short-term security issued in conjunction with a shareholder's preemptive right. The maximum length of a right is 45 days, and it is issued with a subscription price, which allows the holder to purchase the underlying security at a discount from its market price.
rights agent	An independent entity responsible for maintaining the records for rights holders.
rights of accumulation	A right offered to mutual fund investors that allows them to calculate all past contributions and growth to reach a breakpoint to receive a sales charge discount on future purchases.
rights offering	The offering of new shares by a corporation that is preceded by the offering of the new shares to existing shareholders.

riskless simultaneous transaction	The purchase of a security on a principal basis by a brokerage firm for the sole purpose of filling a customer's order that the firm has already received. The markup on riskless principal transactions has to be based on the firm's actual cost for the security.
rollover	The distribution of assets from a qualified account to an investor for the purpose of depositing the assets in another qualified account within 60 days. An investor may only roll over an IRA once every 12 months.
round lot	A standard trading unit for securities. For common and preferred stock, a round lot is 100 shares. For bonds, it is 5 bonds.
Rule 144	SEC rule that regulates the sale of restricted and control securities requiring the seller to file Form 144 at the time the order is entered to sell. Rule 144 also regulates the number of securities that may be sold.
Rule 145	SEC rule that requires a corporation to provide stockholders with full disclosure relating to reorganizations and to solicit proxies.
Rule 147	An intrastate offering that provides an exemption from SEC registration.
Rule 405	The NYSE rule that requires that all customer recommendations must be suitable and that the representative must "know" the customer.

S

sale	See sell.
sales charge	See commission.
sales literature	Written material distributed by a firm to a controlled audience for the purpose of increasing business. Sales literature includes market letters, research reports, and form letters sent to more than 25 customers.
sales load	The amount of commission charged to investors in open-end mutual funds. The amount of the sales load is added to the net asset value of the fund to determine the public offering price of the fund.
satellite office	An office not identified to the public as an office of the member, such as an agent's home office.
savings bond	A nonnegotiable U.S. government bond that must be purchased from the government and redeemed to the government. These bonds are generally known as Series EE and HH bonds.
scale	A list of maturities and yields for a new serial bond issue.
Schedule 13D	A form that must be filed with the SEC by any individual or group of individuals acquiring 5% or more of a corporation's nonexempt equity securities. Form 13D must be filed within 10 days of the acquisition.
scheduled premium policy	A variable life insurance policy with fixed premium payments.
SEC	See Securities and Exchange Commission (SEC).
secondary distribution	A distribution of a large number of securities by a large shareholder or group of large shareholders. The distribution may or may not be done under a prospectus.

secondary offering	An underwriting of a large block of stock being sold by large shareholders. The proceeds of the issue are received by the selling shareholders, not the corporation.
secondary market	A marketplace where securities are exchanged between investors. All transactions that take place on an exchange or on the Nasdaq are secondary market transactions.
sector fund	A mutual fund that invests in companies within a specific business area in an effort to maximize gains. Sector funds have larger risk-reward ratios because of the concentration of investments.
Securities Act of 1933	The first major piece of securities industry legislation. It regulates the primary market and requires that nonexempt issuers file a registration statement with the SEC. The act also requires that investors in new issues be given a prospectus.
Securities Act Amendments of 1975	Created the Municipal Securities Rulemaking Board (MSRB).
Securities Exchange Act of 1934	Regulates the secondary market and all broker dealers and industry participants. It created the Securities and Exchange Commission, the industry's ultimate authority. The act gave the authority to the Federal Reserve Board to regulate the extension of credit for securities purchases through Regulation T.
Securities and Exchange Commission	The ultimate securities industry authority. The SEC is a direct government body, not a self-regulatory organization. The commissioners are appointed by the U.S. President and must be approved by Congress.
Securities Investor Protection Corporation (SIPC)	The industry's nonprofit insurance company that provides protection for investors in case of broker dealer failure. All member firms must pay dues to SIPC based upon their revenue. SIPC provides coverage for each separate customer for up to $500,000, of which a maximum of $250,000 may be cash. The Securities Investor Protection Act of 1970 created SIPC.
security	Any investment that can be exchanged for value between two parties that contains risk. Securities include stocks, bonds, mutual funds, notes, rights, warrants, and options, among others.
segregation	The physical separation of customer and firm assets.
self-regulatory organization (SRO)	An industry authority that regulates its own members. FINRA, the NYSE, and the CBOE are all self-regulatory organizations that regulate their own members.
sell	The act of conveying the ownership of a security for value to another party. A sale includes any security that is attached to another security, as well as any security which the security may be converted or exchanged into.
seller's option	A type of settlement option that allows the seller to determine when delivery of the securities and final settlement of the trade will occur.
selling away	Any recommendation to a customer that involves an investment product that is not offered through the employing firm without the firm's knowledge and consent. This is a violation of industry regulations and may result in action being taken against the representative.
selling concession	See concession.
selling dividends	The act of using a pending dividend to create urgency for the customer to purchase a security. This is a violation and could result in action being taken against the representative.

selling group	A group of broker dealers who may sell a new issue of securities but who are not members of the syndicate and who have no liability to the issuer.
sell out	A transaction executed by a broker dealer when a customer fails to pay for the securities.
sell-stop order	An order placed beneath the current market for a security to protect a profit, to guard against a loss, or to establish a short position.
separate account	The account established by an insurance company to invest the pooled funds of variable contract holders in the securities markets. The separate account must register as either an open-end investment company or as a unit investment trust.
separate trading of registered interest and principal securities (STRIPS)	A zero-coupon bond issued by the U.S. government. The principal payment due in the future is sold to investors at a discount and appreciates to par at maturity. The interest payment component is sold to other investors who want some current income.
serial bonds	A bond issue that has an increasing amount of principal maturing in successive years.
Series EE bond	A nonmarketable U.S. government zero-coupon bond that is issued at a discount and matures at its face value. Investors must purchase the bonds from the U.S. government and redeem them to the government at maturity.
Series HH bond	A nonmarketable U.S. government interest-bearing bond that can only be purchased by trading in matured Series EE bonds. Series HH bonds may not be purchased with cash and are issued with a $500 minimum denomination.
settlement	The completion of a securities transaction. A transaction settles and is completed when the security is delivered to the buyer and the cash is delivered to the seller.
settlement date	The date when a securities ownership changes. Settlement dates are set by FINRA's Uniform Practice Code.
75-5-10 diversification	The diversification test that must be met by mutual funds under the Investment Company Act of 1940 in order to market themselves as a diversified mutual fund: 75% of the fund's assets must be invested in other issuer's securities, no more than 5% of the fund's assets may be invested in any one company, and the fund may own no more than 10% of an issuer's outstanding securities.
shareholder's equity	*See* net worth.
share identification	The process of identifying which shares are being sold at the time the sale order is entered in order to minimize an investor's tax liability.
shelf offering	A type of securities registration that allows the issuer to sell the securities over a 2-year period. Well-known, seasoned issuers may sell securities over a 3-year period.
short	A position established by a bearish investor that is created by borrowing the security and selling in the hopes that the price of the security will fall. The investor hopes to be able to repurchase the security at a lower price, thus replacing it cheaply. If the security's price rises, the investor will suffer a loss.
short against the box	A short position established against an equal long position in the security to roll tax liabilities forward. Most of the benefits of establishing a short against the box position have been eliminated.

short straddle	The simultaneous sale of a call and a put on the same underlying security with the same strike price and expiration. A short straddle would be established by an investor who believes that the security price will move sideways.
simplified arbitration	A method of resolving disputes of $50,000 or less. There is no hearing; one arbitrator reads the submissions and renders a final decision.
Simplified Employee Pension (SEP)	A qualified retirement plan created for small employers with 25 or fewer employees that allows the employees' money to grow tax-deferred until retirement.
single account	An account operated for one individual. The individual has control of the account, and the assets go to the individual's estate in the case of his or her death.
sinking fund	An account established by an issuer of debt to place money for the exclusive purpose of paying bond principal.
special assessment bond	A municipal bond backed by assessments from the property that benefits from the improvements.
specialist	Member of an exchange responsible for maintaining a fair and orderly market in the securities that he or she specializes in and for executing orders left with him or her.
specialist book	A book of limit orders left with the specialist for execution.
special situation fund	A fund that seeks to take advantage of unusual corporate developments, such as takeovers, mergers, and restructuring.
special tax bond	A type of municipal revenue bond that is supported only by revenue from certain taxes.
speculation	An investment objective where the investor is willing to accept a high degree of risk in exchange for the opportunity to realize a high return.
split offering	An offering where a portion of the proceeds from the underwriting goes to the issuer and a portion goes to the selling shareholders.
spousal account	An IRA opened for a nonworking spouse that allows a full contribution to be made for the nonworking spouse.
spread	(1) The difference between the bid and ask for a security. (2) The simultaneous purchase and sale of two calls or two puts on the same underlying security.
spread load plan	A contractual plan that seeks to spread the sales charge over a longer period of time, as detailed in the Spread Load Plan Act of 1970. The maximum sales charge over the life of the plan is 9%, while the maximum sales charge in any one year is 20%.
stabilizing	The only form of price manipulation allowed by the SEC. The managing underwriter enters a bid at or below the offering price to ensure even distribution of shares.
standby underwriting	An underwriting used in connection with a preemptive rights offering. The standby underwriter must purchase any shares not subscribed to by existing shareholders.
statutory disqualification	A set of rules that prohibit an individual who has been barred or suspended or convicted of a securities-related crime from becoming registered.
statutory voting	A method of voting that requires investors to cast their votes evenly for the directors they wish to elect.

stock ahead	A condition that causes an investor's order not to be executed, even though the stock is trading at a price that would satisfy the customer's limit order, because other limit orders have been entered prior to the customer's order.
stock certificate	Evidence of equity ownership.
stock or bond power	A form that, when signed by the owner and attached to a security, makes the security negotiable.
stock split	A change in the number of outstanding shares, the par value, and the number of authorized shares that has been approved through a vote of the shareholders. Forward-stock splits increase the number of shares outstanding and reduce the stock price in order to make the security more attractive to individual investors.
stop limit order	An order that becomes a limit order to buy or sell the stock when the stock trades at or through the stop price.
stop order	An order that becomes a market order to buy or sell the stock when the stock trades at or through the stop price.
stopping stock	A courtesy offered by a specialist to public customers, whereby the specialist guarantees a price but tries to obtain a better price for the customer.
straddle	The simultaneous purchase or sale of a call and a put on the same security with the same strike price and expiration.
straight line depreciation	An accounting method that allows an owner to take equal tax deductions over the useful life of the asset.
strangle	The purchase or sale of a call and a put on either side of the current market price. The options have the same expiration months but different strike prices.
stripped bond	A bond that has had its coupons removed by a broker dealer and that is selling at a deep discount to its principal payment in the future.
stripper well	An oil well that is in operation just to recover a very limited amount of reserves.
subchapter S corporation	A business organization that allows the tax consequences of the organization to flow through to the owners.
subscription agreement	An application signed by the purchaser of an interest in a direct participation plan. An investor in a limited partnership does not become an investor until the general partner signs the subscription agreement.
subscription right	See right.
suitability	A determination that the characteristics of a security are in line with an investor's objectives, financial profile, and attitudes.
Super Display Book System (SDBK)	The electronic order-routing system used by the NYSE to route orders directly to the trading post.
supervise	The actions of a principal that ensure that the actions of a firm and its representatives are in compliance with industry regulations.
support	The price to which a security will fall and attract new buyers. As the new buyers enter the market, it keeps the price from falling any lower.
surplus fund	An account set up for funds generated by a project financed by a municipal revenue bond to pay a variety of expenses.
syndicate	A group of underwriters responsible for underwriting a new issue.

systematic risk	A risk inherent in any investment in the market. An investor may lose money simply because the market is going down.

T

takedown	The price at which a syndicate purchases a new issue of securities from the issuer.
tax and revenue anticipation note	A short-term note sold by a municipal issuer as interim financing in anticipation of tax and other revenue.
tax anticipation note (TAN)	A short-term note sold by a municipal issuer as interim financing in anticipation of tax revenue.
tax-deferred annuity	A nonqualified retirement account that allows an investor's money to grow tax deferred. A tax-deferred annuity is a contract between an insurance company and an investor.
tax equivalent yield	The interest rate that must be offered by a taxable bond of similar quality in order to be equal to the rate that is offered by a municipal bond.
tax-exempt bond fund	A bond fund that seeks to produce investment income that is free from federal tax by investing in a portfolio of municipal bonds.
tax liability	The amount of money that is owed by an investor after realizing a gain on the sale of an investment or after receiving investment income.
tax preference item	An item that receives preferential tax treatment and must be added back into income when calculating an investor's alternative minimum tax.
tax-sheltered annuity (TSA)	A qualified retirement plan offered to employees of governments, school systems, or nonprofit organizations. Contributions to TSAs are made with pre-tax dollars.
technical analysis	A method of security analysis that uses past price performance to predict the future performance of a security.
Telephone Consumer Protection Act of 1991	Legislation that regulates how potential customers are contacted by phone at home.
tenants in common	*See* joint tenants in common.
tender offer	An offer to buy all or part of a company's outstanding securities for cash or cash and securities.
term bond	A bond issue that has its entire principal due on one date.
term maturity	A type of bond maturity that has all principal due on one date.
testimonial	The use of a recognized expert or leader to endorse the services of a firm.
third market	A transaction in an exchange-listed security executed over the Nasdaq workstation.
third-party account	An account that is managed for the benefit of a customer by another party, such as an investment adviser, a trustee, or an attorney.
30-day visible supply	The total par value of all new issue municipal bonds coming to market in the next 30 days.

time deposit	An account that is established by a bank customer where the customer agrees to leave the funds on deposit for an agreed upon amount of time.
time value	The value of an option that exceeds its intrinsic value or its in-the-money amount.
tombstone ad	An announcement published in financial papers advertising the offering of securities by a group of underwriters. Only basic information may be contained in the tombstone ad, and all offers must be made through the prospectus only.
top heavy rule	The rule that states the maximum salary for which a Keogh contribution may be based. This is in effect to limit the disparity between high- and low-salary employees.
trade confirmation	The printed notification of a securities transaction. A confirmation must be sent to a customer on or before the completion of a transaction. The completion of a transaction is considered to be the settlement date.
trade date	The day when an investor's order is executed.
tranche	A class of collateralized mortgage obligation (CMO) that has a predicted maturity and interest rate.
transfer agent	An independent entity that handles name changes, records the names of security holders of record, and ensures that all certificates are properly endorsed.
transfer and hold in safekeeping	A request by customers for the brokerage firm to transfer their securities into the firm's name and to hold them in safekeeping at the firm. A brokerage may charge a fee for holding a customer's securities that have been registered in its name.
transfer and ship	A request by customers for the brokerage firm to transfer their securities into their name and to ship them to their address of record.
Treasury bill	A U.S. government security that is issued at a discount and matures at par in 4, 13, 26, and 52 weeks.
Treasury bond	A long-term U.S. government security that pays semiannual interest and matures in 10 to 30 years.
Treasury note	An intermediate-term U.S. government security that pays semiannual interest and matures in 1 to 10 years.
Treasury receipt	A zero-coupon bond created by a brokerage firm that is backed by U.S. government securities. It is issued at a discount and matures at par.
treasury stock	Stock that has been issued by a corporation and that has subsequently been repurchased by the corporation. Treasury stock does not vote or receive dividends. It is not used in the calculation of earnings per share.
trendline	A line used to predict the future price movement for a security. Drawing a line under the successive lows or successive highs creates a trendline.
trough	The bottoming out of the business cycle just prior to an new upward movement in activity.
true interest cost (TIC)	A calculation for the cost of a municipal issuer's interest expense that includes the time value of money.
Trust Indenture Act of 1940	Regulates the issuance of corporate debt in excess of $10 million and with a term exceeding 1 year. It requires an indenture between the issuer and the trustee.
trustee	A person who legally acts for the benefit of another party.
12B-1 fee	An asset-based distribution fee that is assessed annually and paid out quarterly to cover advertising and distribution costs. All 12B-1 fees must be reasonable.

two-dollar broker	An independent exchange member who executes orders for commission house brokers and other customers for a fee.
type	A classification method for an option as either a call or a put.

U

uncovered	See naked.
underlying security	A security for which an investor has an option to buy or sell.
underwriting	The process of marketing a new issue of securities to the investing public. A broker dealer forwards the proceeds of the sale to the issuer minus its fee for selling the securities.
unearned income	Any income received by an individual from an investment, such as dividends and interest income.
uniform delivery ticket	A document that must be attached to every security delivered by the seller, making the security "good delivery."
Uniform Gifts to Minors Act (UGMA)	Sets forth guidelines for the gifting of cash and securities to minors and for the operation of accounts managed for the benefit of minors. Once a gift is given to a minor, it is irrevocable.
Uniform Practice Code	The FINRA bylaw that sets guidelines for how industry members transact business with other members. The Uniform Practice Code establishes such things as settlement dates, rules of good delivery, and ex-dividend dates.
Uniform Securities Act (USA)	The framework for state-based securities legislation. The act is a model that can be adapted to each state's particular needs.
Uniform Transfer to Minors Act (UTMA)	Legislation that has been adopted in certain states, in lieu of the Uniform Gifts to Minors Act. UTMA allows the custodian to determine the age at which the assets become the property of the minor. The maximum age for transfer of ownership is 25.
unit investment trust (UIT)	A type of investment company organized as a trust to invest in a portfolio of securities. The UIT sells redeemable securities to investors in the form of shares or units of beneficial interest.
unit of beneficial interest	The redeemable share issued to investors in a unit investment trust.
unit refund annuity	An annuity payout option that will make payments to the annuitant for life. If the annuitant dies prior to receiving an amount that is equal to his or her account value, the balance of the account will be paid to the annuitant's beneficiaries.
unqualified legal opinion	A legal opinion issued by a bond attorney for the issue where there are no reservations relating to the issue.
unrealized	A paper profit or loss on a security that is still owned.

V

variable annuity	A contract issued by an insurance company that is both a security and an insurance product. The annuitant's contributions are invested through the separate account into a portfolio of securities. The annuitant's payments depend largely on the investment results of the separate account.
variable death benefit	The amount of a death benefit paid to a beneficiary that is based on the investment results of the insurance company's separate account. This amount is over the contract's minimum guaranteed death benefit.
variable life insurance	A life insurance policy that provides for a minimum guaranteed death benefit, as well as an additional death benefit, based on the investment results of the separate account.
variable rate municipal security	Interim municipal financing issued with a variable rate.
vertical spread	The simultaneous purchase and sale of two calls or two puts on the same underlying security that differ only in strike price.
vesting	The process by which an employer's contributions to an employee's retirement account become the property of the employee.
visible supply	See 30-day visible supply.
voluntary accumulation plan	A method, such as dollar-cost averaging, by which an investor regularly makes contributions to acquire mutual fund shares.
voting right	The right of a corporation's stockholders to cast their votes for the election of the corporation's board of directors as well as for certain major corporate issues.

W

warrant	A long-term security that gives the holder the right to purchase the common shares of a corporation for up to 10 years. The warrant's subscription price is always higher than the price of the underlying common shares when the warrant is initially issued.
wash sale	The sale of a security at a loss and the subsequent repurchase of that security or of a security that is substantially the same within 30 days of the sale. The repurchase disallows the claim of the loss for tax purposes.
western account	A type of municipal security syndicate account where only the member with unsold bonds is responsible for the unsold bonds.
when-issued security	A security that has been sold prior to the certificates being available for delivery.
wildcatting	An exploratory oil- and gas-drilling program.
wire room	See order department.
withdrawal plan	The systematic removal of funds from a mutual fund account over time. Withdrawal plans vary in type and availability among fund companies.
workable indication	An indication of the prices and yields that a municipal securities dealer may be willing to buy or sell bonds.

working capital	A measure of a corporation's liquidity that is found by subtracting current liabilities from current assets.
working interest	An interest that requires the holder to bear the proportional expenses and allows the holder to share in the revenue produced by an oil or gas project in relation to the interest.
workout quote	A nonfirm quote that requires handling and settlement conditions to be worked out between the parties prior to the trade.
writer	An investor who sells an option to receive the premium income.
writing the scale	The procedure of assigning prospective yields to a new issuer of serial municipal bonds.

Y

yield	The annual amount of income generated by a security relative to its price; expressed as a percentage.
yield-based option	An interest rate option that allows the holder to receive the in-the-money amount in cash upon exercise or expiration.
yield curve	The rate at which interest rates vary among investments of similar quality with different maturities. Longer-term securities generally offer higher yields.
yield to call	An investor's overall return for owning a bond should it be called in prior to maturity by the issuer.
yield to maturity	An investor's overall return for owning a bond if the bond is held until maturity.

Z

zero-coupon bond	A bond that is issued at a discount from its par value and makes no regular interest payments. An investor's interest is reflected by the security's appreciation toward par at maturity. The appreciation is taxable each year even though it is not actually received by the investor (phantom income).
zero-minus tick	A trade in an exchange-listed security that occurs at the same price as the previous transaction, but at a price that is lower than the last transaction that was different.
zero-plus tick	A trade in an exchange-listed security that occurs at the same price as the previous transaction, but at a price that is higher than the last transaction that was different.

Made in the USA
Columbia, SC
04 January 2024